Hallowed

Hallowed

Echoes of the Psalms in the Lord's Prayer

REUBEN BREDENHOF

WIPF & STOCK · Eugene, Oregon

HALLOWED
Echoes of the Psalms in the Lord's Prayer

Wipf & Stock
An Imprint of Wipf and Stock Publishers
199 W. 8th Ave., Suite 3
Eugene, OR 97401

www.wipfandstock.com

PAPERBACK ISBN: 978-1-5326-8261-2
HARDCOVER ISBN: 978-1-5326-8262-9
EBOOK ISBN: 978-1-5326-8263-6

Manufactured in the U.S.A.   JUNE 13, 2019

For our daughters

Abigail

Kyra

Sasha

Tori

for whom I am privileged to be an earthly father

while teaching them to know their heavenly Father

Contents

Introduction
Hallowed

IT HAS BEEN SAID that prayer is a lot like breathing. This is a good comparison, because to live, we have to breathe: our bodies simply cannot survive without the constant intake of oxygen. And in the same way, prayer is essential to our spiritual life. To keep going as believers, we need to pray. That is why the Holy Spirit keeps insisting on it, like in 1 Thessalonians 5:17—"Pray without ceasing"—and Ephesians 6:18—"Pray in the Spirit on all occasions with all kinds of prayers and requests" (NIV)—and again in Philippians 4:6—"In everything by prayer and supplication with thanksgiving let your requests be made known to God." The command to continuous prayer reveals how essential it is to our well-being—as indispensable as constant breathing.

Yet if only praying was as easy or natural as breathing! Here that good comparison starts to break down. For when we are in good health, we hardly think about breathing—inhaling and exhaling happen automatically, without effort or concentration. But praying is much harder. It certainly does not come to us naturally. If we don't think about praying, we probably won't do it, and definitely not continually.

Nowadays, prayer also seems outdated and inefficient. Today if we want results, we just send someone a text message or email, or make a quick call from our phone. Prayer—in the sense of taking the time to close our eyes, fold our hands, and talk to God—looks slow and unproductive. Because prayer rarely produces results that are immediate and that are often contrary to what we asked, we begin to wonder if it even works. And the fact is, we do not always know how to do it. Even when we do pray, we sometimes do it badly, with mixed-up priorities, wrong attitudes, and persistent distractions. We know the New Testament injunction to pray "without ceasing," but the habitual nature of our prayers can result in them being hackneyed and human-focused.

All of this means that we should return to passages like Luke 11. The Lord Jesus was praying, and as the disciples listened to their master's words, they must have been impressed by how sincere, complete, and dynamic his prayer was. For "when he finished, one of his disciples said to him, 'Lord, teach *us* to pray'" (v. 1). They wanted him to show how it's done, to give them instruction in what God delights to hear from his people.

In teaching what has come to be called the Lord's Prayer, Jesus mined many themes and phrases directly from the prayers of the Psalms. This Old Testament "Book of Prayer" reveals how God's people approached him in a spirit of worship and trust, petitioned him for life's necessities, confessed their sin, and asked for daily help and guidance. We are still in need of much training in the vital activity of praying, and in this book's fresh study of the Lord's Prayer we will hear its deep echoes of numerous psalms. It is my hope that this resonance can teach us humble and God-centered manners of prayer which will truly hallow the name of our Father in heaven.

This is my second book written to instruct and encourage God's people in the opportunities, challenges, and joys of life in Christ. As with my book on the Ten Commandments and Proverbs (see *Wise: Living by the Ancient Words of the Commandments and Proverbs*, published in 2018), this volume has developed and grown through various iterations, with some of the material being first worked out in a series of sermons to my congregation in Mount Nasura, Western Australia. Much appreciation goes to Marlene de Vos of my congregation, who applied her keen eye for detail to an early draft, finding an embarrassing number of missed words and misplaced commas! In bringing this work to publication, I have also been assisted by Matthew Wimer, Daniel Lanning, and Caleb Shupe at Wipf & Stock, whose professionalism and expertise I greatly value.

My beloved Rebecca has been my chief supporter and encourager for now almost two decades of blessing-filled marriage. For this project she was my astute and meticulous editor once again; I want to thank her too, for suggesting (what I think is) a great title for this book: *Hallowed*. Our gracious Father has entrusted to our care four thoughtful, life-loving, and God-fearing daughters—Abigail, Kyra, Sasha, and Tori. Each of them were happy to read the entire manuscript and to provide their dad with many helpful suggestions, corrections, and even a few compliments. With a father's love and humble gratitude for the heavenly gifts that they are, I dedicate this book to our girls.

Soli Deo Gloria

CHAPTER 1

I Call upon You

The School of Prayer

PSALMS HAS A DEEPLY cherished place among the sixty-six books of the Bible. Perhaps more than any other book in the Scriptures, these are pages opened often and read frequently. This is surely because the Psalms are personal and direct, down-to-earth and true to life, as the authors give an intimate account of their walk with God. Sometimes there is a spirit of great joy in the Psalms, profound thankfulness, and quiet trust. But there can also be sorrow, uncertainty, and fear—even wrenching despair. We can wish that it wasn't so, but these things are definitely real life, too. So we value the authentic voice of the Psalms, appreciating that we can use these ancient words to express in prayer the joys and struggles of walking with God through Jesus his Son. When our own words and earthly perspectives fail us, we find ready help in the book of Psalms.

It is not by accident that this happens. For it was God our Father who gave us this precious book, God who also understands that "we do not know what to pray for as we ought" (Rom 8:26). While we probably think of the Psalms as songs—something akin to today's hymns and praise choruses—many of the Psalms can also be described as *prayers*. For example, there is the heading above Psalm 86, calling it "A Prayer of David" (cf. Pss 17, 90, 102, and 142). Even when they lack this heading, many of the Psalms

1

are records of holy conversations shared between earth and heaven—praise and petitions sent from the child of God to the Lord God himself, revealing the heart of a true relationship with him. In these perfect prayers, we have a shining example of how it can be done. Besides its many other uses in the Christian life, you could call the book of Psalms "a school of prayer."

Teach Us to Pray

During his ministry, the disciples of Jesus asked him about how they could pray. "Teach us," they said, and Jesus did—he taught them the Lord's Prayer (Luke 11:2–4; Matt 6:9–13). It is not elaborate, just six basic petitions, not more than seventy words in most English translations—yet it covers a wide spectrum, concentrating on God's glory and requesting life's daily necessities:

> Our Father in heaven,
> hallowed be your name.
> Your kingdom come,
> your will be done,
> on earth as it is in heaven.
> Give us this day our daily bread,
> and forgive us our debts,
> as we also have forgiven our debtors.
> And lead us not into temptation,
> but deliver us from evil.
> For yours is the kingdom
> and the power
> and the glory,
> forever. Amen.

It is justly considered the perfect prayer. But equally as well, Jesus could have directed his disciples back to the Psalms, the prayer book of God's Old Testament people. It contains essential insights into how to address God, what to ask for, and in what spirit. Indeed, the Lord's Prayer was not an entirely original model for communing with God, for Jesus drew its themes and language in large part from the prayers of the Psalms. His ministry of teaching made it clear that Jesus knew and loved the Psalms (see e.g., Luke 24:44), and when we listen carefully, we notice that his prayer is a pure echo of how God's people have called on him through the Psalms for millennia. Excellent teacher that he was, Jesus drew together these key patterns in order to give a succinct but profound lesson in what delights God when his people pray.

In this chapter, we begin our study of his prayer by pondering a few of the keynotes from the Lord's Prayer and the Psalms. We will use David's prayer in Psalm 86 as our guide for learning about prayer's humble address, its spirit of humility, its core requests, and its sure confidence.

Getting the Address Right

Unless you live in a cave, you've probably sent an email before—and if you have, then you know that the address needs to be right. If you miss even one letter, your message will not arrive where it is intended: it will either bounce back or end up in the inbox of an unsuspecting stranger who probably won't be interested to read about your upcoming team meeting. No matter what you write in the body of the message, the address is critical. The same is true for our prayers: to whom are we sending this message and offering these words? It's not a technicality, like a line of text in an email, but it is a matter of the heart.

This is a crucial component of prayer, for today there are countless multitudes of people who pray. Prayer is not unique to Christians, but is practiced by the followers of many religions. It is even advised by secular psychologists as beneficial to our mental health, so in the self-help sections of many bookstores you can find volumes that promote various methods of prayer. But where are all these prayers going? The Bible says about the gods of the nations: "Their idols are silver and gold, the work of human hands. They have mouths, but do not speak; eyes, but do not see; they have ears, but do not hear" (Ps 115:4–6). If a person addresses their prayer to a false god, it is going to proceed no farther than past the lips. Or if my prayer is mostly aimless ruminating and pious self-talk, it amounts to nothing more than the internal firing of brain synapses—it's certainly not a message that is sent into the heavenly presence of the living God.

Probably very few of this book's readers are in the habit of praying to the gods of wood or stone, gold or plastic. Yet getting the address for our prayers right is still so necessary. With whom are we speaking? What is this God like, whom we approach at the beginning of our day, or at its close, or during one of its many sunny or cloudy moments? Is the Lord distant and unpredictable, an unloving God, or one who is easily annoyed? If the God upon whom we call is any of these things, then our prayers will be useless. If God is cold and aloof, he probably won't care to have fellowship with us, insignificant earthlings. If God is unpredictable, he might listen this time, but not the next—if unloving, he might scorn the pathetic things that you and I struggle with every day. But if God is kind and gracious and ready to listen, then we can speak to him in trust, expectation, and gratitude.

The opening words of a prayer can speak volumes then, for they can reveal what we think of God and what kind of relationship we have with him. Are we casual and nonchalant in his presence? Do we treat God like someone who is waiting to cater to all our needs and respond to our troubles? Or are we simply glad to seek him in prayer and to enjoy his loving presence? Do we trust him wholeheartedly, bow before his holy grandeur, and worship him with our words? A proper address is the first and essential building-block that we need in order to start forming a prayer that pleases God.

The Inclined Ear

In Psalm 86, David shows how to address God in a spirit of affection and expectation. He wrote this prayer about a situation of trouble that he was facing; we don't know the exact circumstances, but it's evident that he was distressed by a band of brash enemies

(v. 14). These enemies hated David, and his life was threatened by their violence. Various possibilities can be imagined from the narratives of 1 and 2 Samuel, such as when he was pursued through the wilderness by King Saul, who saw him as a threat to his rule, or when David's rebellious son Absalom later attempted to seize the throne of Israel.

Whatever the circumstance, David knows that he can look for help to the one true God. From his prayer's first line, that is what he does: "Incline your ear, O LORD, and hear me" (v. 1). While God is spirit and does not have ears (or hands or eyes or a mouth), this image of an inclined ear—picture a parental head tilted in concern toward a little child voicing her fears—distinctly expresses the hope that God will notice our prayers. The gods of the nations lack hearing ears (Ps 115:6), but God surely pays loving attention to the voice of his people.

This first verse is the crucial address that David affixes to his prayer: "O LORD . . . answer me." Who is the LORD? We know him from the rest of Scripture: the LORD (which is often spelled with all capital letters in English translations) is *Yahweh*, the faithful God of the covenant of grace. This should be distinguished from "Lord," another name for God which recurs throughout Psalm 86 as a translation of the Hebrew name *Adonai* (see vv. 3, 4, 8, 9), a name that emphasizes God's power and sovereignty. In his prayer's address in verse 1, David refers to the LORD, the same one who gave precious promises to Abraham, Isaac, and Jacob (Exod 3:15). The LORD is the God who never forsakes or abandons his covenant people; he is the one who has joined himself to us by a sacred oath in the blood of Christ (Heb 7:13–15). When we echo David's prayer and call on the LORD (*Yahweh*), we are talking to the God who is by definition true, faithful, and trustworthy.

Sometimes parents will caution their children as they head out to the neighborhood park, "Don't talk to strangers!" The unknown is frightening and potentially harmful. Even when we're older, we can be wary of approaching people whom we don't know, because we cannot be sure how they'll react to us. But God is no stranger; we are allowed to talk to him because we have a relationship with him through Christ his Son. He has become our heavenly Father, so we can address him with a sure confidence, praying along with David: "Incline your ear, O LORD, and answer me."

On that same basis of reverent familiarity, David boldly declares in verse 2, "You are my God." Ponder that little word "my," reflecting on what it means for prayer. It speaks of the bond that we enjoy with God, the connection that makes intimate this holy conversation. He is *our* heavenly Father! We didn't choose God, he chose us, and in a marvelous way he has given himself to us as our own. So we can say every time we pray, "In Christ, you are my God. You're the one I look to. Lord, you have promised to help me—so please hear my voice."

Adverbs and Adjectives

We have been saying that David prays to God because he *knows* God. For David there is no uncertainty: he knows that God will hear his request and that he will do something about it, because he is the God of grace. David prays, "Be gracious to me, O Lord" (v. 3). As David stands on the brink of disaster, it is the merciful and compassionate God who fills his vision. This is always the heart of a true prayer, when a child of God approaches him in the recognition that his mercy and undeserved compassion are our greatest need.

We sometimes act as if God's grace is more supplemental than essential. Grace is our fallback position, something reserved for times of serious disruption and turmoil when we have really run stuck or especially messed up. But even as we start a new and entirely ordinary day, we should realize the true depths of our poverty. Every day we ought to pray: "Be gracious to me, O Lord. In your grace help me to be faithful, whatever blessing you send, whatever trouble you send. My God, I need you every hour."

And when this is our sincere prayer, we can have the confidence that God will show grace! For this is who God is: "You, O Lord, are good and forgiving, abounding in steadfast love to all who call upon you" (v. 5). In his amazement before the Lord,

David piles up the adverbs and adjectives. He does it again in verse 15, where he prays, "You, O Lord, are a God full of compassion, and gracious, longsuffering and abundant in mercy and truth." Though he is swimming in dire straits, David resolves to hallow God's name, and he does so by resting himself in the kind and faithful character of God.

God already knows how great he is, so he certainly doesn't need to hear it from us. Compare it to hiking through some mountainous terrain and standing in humble awe before the majestic snowcapped peaks. They have been there for thousands of years, and they will be there long after we're gone. The mountains don't need us to comment on their beauty or snap a photo any more than the eternal God needs us to recognize him. But he wants us to! He wants to hear it from us because he is so deserving of humble and awe-inspired worship. This is the aim of the first petition of the Lord's prayer, "Hallowed be your name," which we'll explore in a subsequent chapter. Jesus teaches us to pray with a spirit that yearns to hallow and sanctify and glorify the Father: "In this day, in this world, and in all my life, may your perfect beauty and unfailing goodness be evident!"

Reflecting on the shortcomings of my own prayers, I wonder if other believers really celebrate God's exalted character when they approach him. Do we pause and meditate on the greatness and goodness of the God with whom we are speaking? Or do we overlook that activity, keep the address line as short as possible, and start uploading our long list of concerns, wishes, and troubles? Do we remember to hallow his name? We must, for God is so eminently worthy of worship and adoration! As the twenty-four elders cry out to him in Revelation 4:11, "Worthy are you, our Lord and God, to receive glory and honor and power, for you created all things, and by your will they existed and were created."

It can actually be a vigorous boost to our prayer to know that we are approaching a God who is so great and holy and worthy. Even in the midst of his trouble, David rejoices to make this confession: "There is none like you among the gods, O Lord, nor are there any works like yours" (v. 8). Sincerely voicing words like that can change our outlook, for praise makes us more conscious of God's illustrious splendor; it encourages us to know that this great God is very near. Reverential praise draws our vision away from ourselves and our daily fears, and it reminds us that we have come into the presence of almighty God. Our concerns might be ordinary and down-to-earth, but true prayer elevates us into the throne room of heaven. What do I have to worry about? Why am I troubled? The Lord is my God, and there is none like him!

The Humility of Neediness

When David writes Psalm 86, he does not hide his helplessness. He puts it on a banner at the very beginning: "Incline your ear, O LORD, and answer me, for I am poor and needy" (v. 1). Sometimes we describe a person who we know as "needy" because they always need extra attention and support. In our books, "needy" is not a compliment. We wish people could be more independent and could get on without receiving so much help.

David's confession of need is definitely not about money, for he was the king of Israel and had access to great wealth, abundant resources, and a formidable army. But the Holy Spirit helps David to see things as they really are, to realize that at the bottom he is truly destitute and incapable. He prays from a position of lowliness before God, which is a necessary posture for every believer who wants to pray meaningfully. As sinners, we ought to acknowledge to God that we are too weak to resist the devil, too ignorant to discern God's will, and too frail to endure past tomorrow, for we are "poor and needy."

When you are truly poor and needy, you can only ask for a freebie and plead for charity. Praying in that spirit is not easy, for we are often deluded by a prideful self-assurance. But if we think that we're doing fine, and we don't acknowledge that we need his help, we can hardly expect God to come near and answer. Similarly, if we don't consider ourselves to be terribly sinful or guilty, why should God forgive? Jesus promises that God's mercy is for those who know themselves to be poor when they call on him. For instance, in his Sermon on the Mount, he announces, "Blessed are the poor in spirit, for theirs is the kingdom of heaven" (Matt 5:3). A prayer is acceptable if it is offered in this kind of humility before God. Whenever we pray, in whatever situation of our life—favorable or miserable or just normal—we should remind ourselves of the fundamental truth: "God opposes the proud, but gives grace to the humble" (1 Pet 5:5).

Structural Humility

God-pleasing humility is not just something we can add to our prayer perfunctorily, like a dash of salt to a fried egg. In prayer, humility should be *structural*, part of the very shape and composition of all the words we send up to God—where our praises and petitions are marked by a multifaceted lowliness of spirit.

We can express this spirit in various ways. For instance, an attitude of humility should permeate our praise when we stand impressed by God's sovereign majesty and unfailing goodness. Like David demonstrates with all the adverbs and adjectives of Psalm 86, God's glory should regularly amaze us and cause us to exclaim, "Who am I, that this great God should think of me? Who am I, that I may call upon the Lord of heaven and earth?" (see 2 Sam 7:18). We are sinners and mortals, like weak sheep or lowly earthworms, but God is the mighty and heavenly and holy king—so in lowliness we glorify the Lord through prayer.

Humility in prayer is also expressed through our confession of sin; in another chapter, we will see how that is the point of Jesus's fifth petition: "Forgive us our debts." Offering such a petition means we do not generalize or minimize our sin. Rather, God wants us to come clean in confession, being as specific as we can be about our shortcomings and transgressions. Then we humbly ask for his forgiveness in Christ's name, praying with this confidence: "You, O Lord, are good and forgiving" (Ps 86:5).

Our humility before God is perhaps most apparent when we simply and truly ask for help. This is what the courageous and mighty King David says in Psalm 86:1 ("I am poor and needy")

and again in verse 7 ("In the day of my trouble I call upon you").
He does not hesitate to admit that he is in trouble, that God is his
only help, his first and last hope—his lifeline. Can we echo David's
words and agree that prayer is usually our earliest response? When
we face any challenge or trouble, significant or slight, is it our holy
instinct to kneel and pray? Is prayer the first thing we do when we
start a day, and do we seek God's help and direction for whatever
task he has given? Or is it only later that we pray—when we've
dug deep and come up empty? Do we pray only when we've tried
everything else?

If you're a human being, you are desperately needy and you
need to pray: "Listen to my plea for grace" (Ps 86:6). And when
you pray, God *will* give grace, answering and helping you. For the
sake of the crucified Jesus, God comes near those who are needy.
Christ used to be rich, yet for our sakes he became poor, so that we
can receive all the treasures of his salvation (2 Cor 8:9)! In Christ,
you have free access to the riches of God's love—so you should
realize your need, humbly confess it, and then be richly satisfied
in him.

Essential Requests

Sometimes it feels like our prayers are an incessant flood of requests: "Father, please grant me . . . Be near to so-and-so . . . Bless
me in this . . . Protect my family from . . ." In Psalm 86, we witness something similar, for again and again—fourteen times by
my count—David presents his urgent requests to God. He asks
for things like God's listening ear, his answer, his preservation,
his grace, a renewal of joy, the Lord's teaching and guidance, his
strength, and a sign of his favor. Put together, these rapid-fire
requests highlight the danger that David is facing as one who is
"poor and needy" (v. 1). At the same time, all these requests reveal
the sure confidence that David has in God as the one who is willing to receive and answer every plea of his people.

David's leading petition is in verse 2, a request that summa-
rizes everything that he will ask for in this prayer. He says to God,

"Preserve my life." This is a simple but loaded petition. It is not a request for extras and frills, but David asks for everything essential that he needs to live. In like manner, we can ask of God in prayer: "Preserve my life. All that I am today, and all the days of my future—please take care of this. Where I am in danger, guard me. Where I am lacking, provide for me. Where I am broken, please restore me. Uphold my life!" This is another key lesson to learn from the Psalms and the Lord's Prayer: we don't need to restrict ourselves to making timid and trivial requests of God, but we can boldly ask for *all* the things that we need for body and soul. When we pray in humility through Jesus, we are assured that the Father will grant his mercy, his Holy Spirit, and every good thing that we truly require (Luke 11:13).

One of David's primary concerns in this prayer is that he would be protected from enemies. He complains to God in verse 14: "Insolent men have risen up against me; a band of ruthless men seeks my life." David has heard the rattling of the swords, he has seen the evil glint in their eyes, and he knows they will show no mercy. Now, it is possible that Christians in your country are not facing violent assaults or angry mobs—thank God for this mercy! Nonetheless, the church has sworn enemies, and in these last days, we see more clearly than ever that they are pitted against the followers of Christ. They don't just hold something against us personally; as David says to God, these men "do not set *you* before them" (v. 14). This teaches us that the church isn't opposed or ridiculed today simply because of our socially-unacceptable views; this hostility is ultimately an opposition to the true God himself.

We pray for preservation from anti-Christian forces, but we should also realize that God might not keep us from harm or shield us from mockery. In fact, we know that it is going to come: persecution is Christ's promise (see Matt 10:16–25; 2 Tim 3:12). But we pray for strength to be faithful, not to surrender or compromise; we ask God to uphold us in his power and grant the courage to resist. Today we pray, "Preserve my life, O Lord, and deliver me from those who are busy waging war against your kingdom and your people." Later in this book, we'll see that this is the keynote of the sixth petition, "Lead us not into temptation, but deliver us from evil." Both David and Jesus teach us to pray for God to maintain us by his power and keep us from being overwhelmed by spiritual foes.

Another essential request taught by David is in verse 11: "Teach me your way, O LORD, that I may walk in your truth." Because of his perilous situation, David is confused and perplexed. He doesn't say exactly what kind of direction he is seeking from God: guidance on how to respond to his enemies' accusations, or what is the best military strategy to use, or how to lead his family or nation in this time of strife. But he acknowledges his ignorance and asks for insight into God's will.

It remains true that if our life will flourish in God's service, then we need to know his way and will. How does God want you to treat your parents, your teachers, or your workplace manager? What is his wisdom for your weekend activities, for your spending at the shopping mall, or for your use of digital technology? How can you deal appropriately with this difficult relationship in your congregation or family? We pray for God to preserve our life from the confusion that sin always produces, to help us overcome our natural ignorance of God's wisdom: "Teach me your way, O LORD, that I may walk in your truth." Later we will see that this, too, is akin to what Jesus teaches in the third petition of his prayer, "Your will be done," a request that we would know and do God's will in all things.

Humble Yet Confident

Running throughout David's prayer in Psalm 86 is a strong current of faith. His confidence is so strong that he is not even afraid to predict what God will do. This is what David knows: God will hear his prayer and do something about it. He affirms, "In the day of my trouble I call upon you, for you answer me" (v. 7). David is deeply humble, cognizant of his total neediness before the Lord, yet he is—almost paradoxically—immensely confident.

As we said before, David has such assurance in prayer because he knows the God whom he is addressing. He has learned God's covenant promises and experienced what the Lord can do. He knows for certain that God is faithful, merciful, compassionate, powerful, and ever-present. More than simply grasping these truths in his head, David embraces this God with his heart, praying in faith: "Save your servant, who *trusts* in you" (v. 2). Even if David finds himself at the pointy end of his enemy's sword, he will trust in God. Even in disaster, he is certain that God has not ignored his words, and he is assured that God's answer will be good.

We can offer our prayers in the same blessed assurance, trusting God to hear us for Christ's sake. When we call, God answers. When we ask him according to his will, God supplies. We don't know *how* the answer will come or *when*, but we can always begin with the prayer of faith. If we are praying today, we can know that God will never turn us away or forsake us, but through Jesus he will graciously come near (John 14:13–14). Even if we are disappointed by God's present answer to our prayers, we can keep praying. Even if we wonder how this painful outcome fits into God's good plan for our life, we can commit our way to him. The Lord might have steered us into a misery like David was experiencing in Psalm 86—or laid on us a burden that seems far worse—but we can rest ourselves in God's steadfast character, continuing to pray with a sure confidence in Christ. Even in our darkest hour, we can be assured that the Father will incline his ear and hear us.

Reflection and Discussion Questions

1. Do you have a favorite psalm? Why is it your favorite? Study it to consider whether you can offer any elements of it to God as a prayer.

2. How do you typically begin your prayers? Do you think that there is a need to build more praise into your prayers? How could you do so?

3. How should praying in the name of Christ give you great confidence? (See Heb 10:19–22.)

4. Would you describe yourself as needy, like David does? Why or why not? In what areas of your life do you most clearly see your poverty?

5. Can you relate to the situation that David faced in Psalm 86, "insolent men" rising up against him? When? Why? What was your response?

6. How does Christ's teaching in Luke 11:9–13 encourage you in prayer?

CHAPTER 2

My Father in Heaven

Extraordinary Privilege

DURING HIS EARTHLY MINISTRY, Jesus spoke many extraordinary words, and one of the most remarkable things he said pertained to prayer. He gave permission to human beings to address God as "our Father in heaven" (Matt 6:9). Christians are well-accustomed to that privilege, of course, so it can happen that we pray the Father's name thoughtlessly or mechanically. "Father" might punctuate our prayers from beginning to end: "Father . . . Father . . . Father . . . " But hear how Jesus describes this miracle in Matthew 11: "No one knows the Son except the Father, and no one knows the Father except the Son and anyone to whom the Son chooses to reveal him" (v. 27). Whenever we pray and take the name of God the Father on our lips, it is only because Christ has graciously chosen to reveal him to us. Jesus teaches that when we pray "Father," we are doing something incredibly bold and at the same time deeply reassuring.

That it is such a gift is also clear from what Jesus says in the preceding verses of Matthew 11, "I thank you, Father, Lord of heaven and earth, that you have hidden these things from the wise and understanding and revealed them to little children" (v. 25). He is saying that not everyone can call on the Father, and some don't even understand the significance of this privilege—it is something in which the proud of heart cannot share. But through Christ and by his Holy Spirit, God's little children can pray lovingly and sincerely to their Father in heaven.

Whenever we use this extraordinary address, God says that we can have a child-like attitude, looking to him with the eyes of a child (Ps 131:1–2; Matt 18:2–4). Instead of taking it for granted, we must be awakened to the beautiful truth that when we believe in him, the living God calls us his own children through Christ. God desires us to be his humbly trusting sons and daughters in prayer and in all of life. In this chapter we'll see that, as with each part of the Lord's Prayer, Jesus drew the spirit of the "our Father" address from the Old Testament prayers in the Psalms. Yet we'll also see that, for more than any other aspect of Christ's prayer, in the New Testament there is an amazing deepening of this revelation of God as our Father.

Approaching the King

Years ago, one of the young women in the church that I was pastoring was given the opportunity to meet Queen Elizabeth II when she came to our city on a Commonwealth tour. This young sister soon learned that this was a great privilege about which she could not be careless. There is a highly-developed protocol involved in meeting the Queen: you must first make a bow or a curtsy, you must always refer to her as "Your Majesty," and you must not talk to her unless she first addresses you. And whatever you do, don't touch her! We might judge these royal protocols to be overdone, yet they highlight her venerable position; it is impossible to be in her presence and to forget that this diminutive senior citizen is queen of the United Kingdom and the other Commonwealth realms.

This tradition of reverence offers a good lesson about approaching God in prayer. Now, it is true that we no longer need to be preoccupied with outward ceremony and protocol when drawing near to the Lord. Since the one sacrifice of Jesus, we can come to God freely, "with a true heart in full assurance of faith" (Heb 10:22). Yet associated with that precious gift of freedom is the serious danger of lowering the Lord to our level, making him a little more like a human and a little less like God. Whenever we approach him, we must beware of forgetting that he is the king. Each time we pray, do we stand in wonder at who God is as the Creator of heaven and earth, as the triune God, our Savior and Lord? Or do we like to think of God in our own terms, perhaps conceiving of him as little more than a superpowered friend, or someone like an all-knowing therapist or a good-natured grandparent? Such an attitude dishonors him, and if we lower him at all, we profane his holy name. It is therefore with good reason that Christ teaches us to address God—as our Father, yes—but as our Father who is *in heaven.* This is a powerful pointer to the sovereign majesty that God possesses; it is a profound revelation that the God to whom we are praying is enthroned in heavenly glory and wants to be approached with reverent awe.

Heavenly Majesty

Scripture often reveals the heavenly majesty of God. One outstanding example is in Psalm 103, where David's first instinct is to give glory to God. Praise leaps off the page in verse 1: "Bless the LORD, O my soul"—this adoration is amplified in verse 2: "Bless the LORD, O my soul, and forget not all his benefits"—and worship saturates every verse that follows. David reprises his worshipful theme near the ending of the psalm when he cries, "Bless the LORD, all his works, in all places of his dominion. Bless the LORD, O my soul!" (v. 22).

Psalm 103 is certainly about the marvelous things that God has accomplished for the good of his people. But even more fundamentally, this psalm is about God's greatness in himself, his inherent glory as the mighty Lord. Consider how God's greatness is expressed in verse 19: "The LORD has established his throne in the heavens, and his kingdom rules over all." David tells everyone to look to heaven, for that's where God is and where God reigns from his exalted throne.

For those who have been brought up learning about the Bible, this is probably nothing new. If you ask a child in your church about heaven, she'll likely point up to the clouds: "Sure, that's where God lives!" We smile at the simplicity of children, yet we struggle to understand what it means. Part of the problem is defining what or where this "heaven" is. It is not the same as you can say for Queen Elizabeth II: "Her home is at Buckingham Palace, London, England." When it comes to God and his throne, there is no such geographic precision. And the location of heaven is something that has often been misunderstood. It is reported that the first man in space, a Russian cosmonaut back in the 1960s, radioed back to earth once he was up in the earth's orbit, "I don't see any God up here." He was in "heaven," but there was no God to be found!

Scripture teaches that, although God makes his dwelling "in heaven," he is not limited to that particular locale. God is spirit, so it's not as if he can only be in heaven and not be present anywhere else. Think of how King Solomon was humbled by this truth when he prayed at the dedication of the temple in Jerusalem, seven years in the making: "But will God indeed dwell on the earth? Behold, heaven and the highest heaven cannot contain you; how much less this house that I have built!" (1 Kgs 8:27). God in his glory is exalted above the highest heights of creation, beyond even the farthest reaches of the universe! From his heavenly throne, the Lord rules all things according to his wise purpose.

"Heaven Help Us!"

At the end of Psalm 103, there is a resounding climax where David summons all creation to bow before God's glorious majesty. He begins with heaven, inviting the king's angelic servants to praise him: "Bless the LORD, O you his angels, you mighty ones who do his word, obeying the voice of his word!" (v. 20). David here pictures the heavenly throne room where God is surrounded by multitudes of his most powerful creatures (cf. Isa 6:1–3). These are the mighty angels who worship God endlessly, the heavenly servants who faithfully carry out his will on earth: conveying his messages, defending his people, and moving the kings and populations of mankind.

Such a glimpse into his brilliant throne-room reveals that when we prayerfully address God "in heaven," this is not about God residing in some precise location. Instead, it is a window into how majestic, powerful, and sovereign is the Lord God. Recall what David gladly confesses in this psalm: "The LORD has established his throne in the heavens" (v. 19). From God's high and lofty throne, he rules all creation. He speaks and the sky pours down rain; he gives the order and the tectonic plates begin to shift; he issues commands and his angels fulfill them on earth without delay. God in heaven has limitless resources and supreme power, together with the willingness to use them for our good.

People will sometimes cry out in moments of distress, "Heaven help us!" Such a petition surely arises from the awareness that "heaven" *can* help, that the God enthroned above really can do all things. This childlike simplicity is good, for young children happily accept that God is in heaven; though they have not seen him, they believe in him. They know what their Father can do, and they don't doubt it for a second. Scripture teaches that our prayers can be offered in the same trusting manner, certain that God can manage and direct every circumstance of our life—even if we have no idea how or when or for what purpose. We can pray in humble awe of his glory, with a confidence that the unseen, unsearchable, and unshakable God in heaven truly is our Father.

An Old Name

The key premise of this book is that the Lord's Prayer wasn't a newfangled invention of Jesus, but each petition echoes the ancient prayers recorded in the Psalms. This is true also for the address of his prayer, when Jesus teaches us to call on God as "Father." For a long time now, God's people have known something about his fatherly care. This is evident in the repeated references to God as Father in the Old Testament. For instance, we find this name for God in the Song of Moses in Deuteronomy 32. Here Moses asks the people, "*Is not he your father*, who created you, who made you and established you?" (v. 6). From the way in which Moses asks the question, you can tell he expects a positive answer: "Undoubtedly, God *is* our Father!" God is Israel's Father because he created them in his image and then saved them through his mercy—by his own gracious doing, the children of Abraham became the Lord's family. God once sent this message to Pharaoh: "'Israel is my firstborn son,' and I say to you, 'Let my son go that he may serve me'" (Exod 4:22–23). Because God claimed Israel for himself, as a protective Father, he was willing to deliver his children with his mighty hand and outstretched arm.

For their part, the Israelites knew that within a household, the father is the head of the family, and his children are called to honor and obey him in all good things. A father's holy task is to lead and shape his children in a God-pleasing way. In this regard, too, the heavenly God is a Father to his people because he teaches and nurtures his sons and daughters—while also expecting us to submit humbly.

Isaiah compares God's fatherly shaping of Israel to the way in which a potter will sculpt his clay. A potter begins with a lump of raw material on his wheel or his table. As it sits there, that clay is formless, even useless, without purpose or beauty. But the potter has a plan for the finished product, and the clay is his to shape, so he starts to work. He bends, flattens, smooths, and removes until the clay begins to resemble a jar or plate or some other vessel. Such is the manner in which God the Father works on his people; Isaiah confesses, "But now, O LORD, *you are our Father*; we are the clay, and you are our potter; we are all the work of your hand" (64:8). He speaks of God's total freedom as Creator and Lord; the Father is free to do whatever he pleases, molding a person according to his design, shaping them so that they'll have purpose and beauty in his eyes. Still today, if you're listening, the Father is teaching you through his Holy Spirit. If you're reading, he is guiding you through his word. If you're paying attention, the Father is forming you through the care of godly friends and through the experiences of life, for he wants you to grow. You are the work of his hand.

The Father's Relentless Love

When we survey the revelation of God as Father in the Old Testament, we should also consider the Father's discipline. "My son, do not despise the LORD's discipline or be weary of his reproof," Solomon says in Proverbs, "for the LORD reproves him whom he loves, *as a father the son in whom he delights*" (3:11–12). It is because he delights in us that God unsettles us when we stray, or challenges us when there is something we need to learn. Just like a loving father, he corrects his children through the hardships he sends, through prayers that he seems to leave unanswered, through the trials of home and the struggles of health. This isn't vindictive punishment, it is the Father's gracious forming—experienced for centuries by God's covenant people, and still experienced by us (Heb 12:3–11).

While God's fatherly discipline is almost effortless for me to write about, it is grueling for his people to experience. Even so, God is the Father who unrelentingly loves his children and whose treatment of us is marked by untiring mercy. For instance, the Holy Spirit reveals in Psalm 68:5 that God is a "*father of the fatherless* and protector of widows*." God has special care for those who are weak, vulnerable, and overwhelmed in their suffering. If you're crying out under his discipline, you can be sure that the Father's ear is open to you. This is similar to the heartening picture of God in Deuteronomy 1:31; Moses is speaking to Israel as they wait outside the promised land, and he reminds them: "You have seen how the LORD your God carried you, *as a man carries his son*, all the way that you went until you came to this place." When Israel was utterly feeble during their wilderness journeys, when they were threatened and hungry and even being chastised for their sin, God did for them what any loving father would: he carried his son Israel and brought him to safety. Such is the tender and faithful love of God our Father!

Fatherly Compassion

Among the several Old Testament passages that reveal God as Father, Psalm 103 probably shines brightest: *"As a father shows compassion to his children,* so the LORD shows compassion to those who fear him"* (v. 13). David had the keen sense of God as Father because he was someone who walked with God, daily experiencing his gracious character and loving treatment. For instance, David knew firsthand that God is a Father "who forgives all your iniquity, who heals all your diseases, who redeems your life from the pit, who crowns you with steadfast love and mercy" (vv. 3–4). David brought confessions of sin to God in Psalms 32 and 51, for at times he broke God's laws terribly and shamefully. He felt the misery of guilt as it eroded his peace and tormented his body, but after a period of discipline, he experienced again the Lord's forgiving grace, tasting the profound relief that comes when God shows mercy. David is so glad that God the Father shows compassion and pities those who fear him; he gratefully announces that the Lord "forgives all your iniquity" (v. 3) and does not "keep his anger forever" (v. 9).

If not for God's gracious temperament toward sinners, we would be completely lost. For if God is always an affectionate Father, then we are recalcitrant children: strong-willed, stubborn, sometimes shocking in our ingratitude. Like children often do, we live in the moment, surrendering to impulse even if it leads to terrible results for ourselves and for others. We reject the Father's wise guidance, though it means hurting the one who cares the most. Even so, for Christ's sake, God is a patient and compassionate Father, "slow to anger and abounding in steadfast love" (v. 8).

David's song of joy in Psalm 103 also praises the Lord for being the one "who redeems your life from the pit" (v. 4). Pursued by his enemies and fearing for his life, more than once David was as good as dead and sunk in despair. He certainly had been in "the pit," recounting its misery in places like Psalms 56 and 57. But every time again, the Father extended his strong hand, pulled him out and redeemed his life; from his own experience, David knew how true it is that God "crowns you with steadfast love and mercy" (Ps 103:4). The Father's care for his children is constant.

What makes God's fatherly goodness and kindness even more remarkable is that they're not merited; David sings, "He does not deal with us according to our sins, nor repay us according to our iniquities" (v. 10). To some extent, a child of God is aware of the appalling punishment that sin deserves, so to receive an abundance of good things instead is entirely a gift of the Lord's grace! A child of God can rejoice that God is a father who has boundless mercy on his children, whose steadfast love is "as high as the heavens are above the earth" (v. 11).

A Newer and Deeper Meaning

David sang his hymn of praise in Psalm 103 because he knew God's rich love. So do we—in fact, through the cross of Jesus, we know God's grace even more concretely and memorably than David ever did. In several places, the Old Testament hints at the privilege of knowing and addressing God as Father, but through the work of Christ and his Spirit, we are allowed to enjoy this privilege fully. The New Testament reveals that this is how much the Father loves us, that he gave his only Son to die for sinners (John 3:16). David sang and prayed because he was safe in God's forgiving and restoring love—we are safe too, and we know the cost of this safety! Says Paul, "When the fullness of time had come, God sent forth his Son, born of woman, born under the law, to redeem those who were under the law, so that we might receive adoption as sons" (Gal 4:4–5). Christ, the true Son of God, lived in full obedience to his Father and was faithful even unto death. And God was well-pleased with him, so pleased that God now welcomes believers into his heavenly household, and he gives us permission to call him "Father."

During his ministry and life, Jesus showed what our heavenly Father is like, demonstrating that God is dependable, gracious, and mighty. Jesus always loved and trusted his Father, which is why, as he suffered in the garden of Gethsemane, desperate in his longing for support and help, Jesus turned to him with these words: he prayed, "Abba, Father, all things are possible for you" (Mark 14:36). In his hour of greatest need, he needed to be in the presence of his loving Father.

Now we can call on God in the same way that Jesus did in the garden, with the same closeness and confidence as the Son of God himself. As Paul continues to explain in Galatians 4, "Because you are sons, God has sent the Spirit of his Son into our hearts, crying, 'Abba, Father!'" (v. 6). Through his Holy Spirit working within, our Savior teaches us to call on the Father in true faith. When we go to him, there is no need for fear or uncertainty, for God gives us permission to pray with resolute confidence, "Our Father who is in heaven—Father, all things are possible for you."

The Father who Understands

When we pray to our Father in Christ, God will show mercy, particularly because he understands our frail condition. Remember Psalm 103: "As a father shows compassion to his children, so the LORD shows compassion to those who fear him. For he knows our frame; he remembers that we are dust" (vv. 13–14). The Father recognizes the lowliness of our state and understands what we need, so he pities us and cares for us.

This is a mark of loving and attentive parents, that they know their children—"they know their frame"—what they're made of. Parents can generally see when their kids are tired, when they've had a rough day at school, or when they're feeling grouchy. So parents will try hard to fight against their own impatience and frustration and cut the kids a little slack. They might give an extra hug, speak words of kindness, or maybe they'll agree that it's a good idea to have dessert tonight. When parents see the weakness and worry of their children, they try to make things better. Psalm 103 says that God is a Father who sees the infirmity of his children from a mile away. It's a rich comfort that he knows our frame, comprehending exactly where we've come from in life, the good and the bad that we've been through. The Father understands that no matter how strong or capable or confident we appear on the outside, we are intrinsically weak: physically, emotionally, and spiritually weak. Because Christ his Son can relate to our sufferings and sympathetically intercedes for us (Heb 4:15–16), the Father understands perfectly our earthly condition, and he responds in wisdom and compassion.

Great Expectations

While writing this chapter, it was on my mind how some believers have a hard time looking to God as Father because of what their earthly fathers were like. No father is perfect, but some children have suffered much from an unloving father, an ungodly father, or even an abusive father. In Scripture, too, we see how some of the holiest men failed badly in this role. Think of Noah, Abraham, and David himself, who set poor examples, showed favoritism, and were lax in discipline. Such fatherly failures are seen in Scripture and still witnessed in the church today.

So a weary soul might ask, "God is Father? That means he'll never have a kind word for me. It means he'll only teach me his bad habits. And this Father will likely fail me when I need him the most." Probably all of us can think of our earthly fathers and mention their failings, but this doesn't allow us to think any less of God our Father. For then we have it backwards: our earthly fathers aren't examples for God the Father in heaven, but God the Father must be an example for them! This is the high standard for every Christian father today, that our character must reflect the holy character of God the Father in heaven, who is unfailingly merciful, patient, faithful, and wise.

As children of God, we have immense consolation in the character of our heavenly Father and the steadfast promises of his word. David powerfully voices this assurance in Psalm 27: "Though my father and mother forsake me, the LORD will receive me" (v. 10, NIV). There might come a time in our life when we feel utterly alone, when our earthly securities fall away, and every personal support proves to be unreliable. Even then, we can pray in the complete confidence that our Father will always take care of us: in love, in kindness, in perfect understanding. For he is our Father, and he is in heaven.

How Deep the Father's Love for Us

It is remarkable how much Christ can teach through the few words of his prayer's address. He teaches us to expect everything we need from God in heaven, for "the steadfast love of the LORD is from everlasting to everlasting on those who fear him, and his righteousness to children's children" (Ps 103:17). For as long as we need it, even for times that are everlasting, the Father will love us as his very own! As you lay your life before him in prayer each day, be awakened to this reality: the almighty and heavenly God is your Father through Christ Jesus. The Father has eyes to see you, ears to hear you, a voice to teach, and hands to help. The Father is very near, and he is strong to save—so, each day, he wants to hear your childlike prayers, however small or simple they might be. In Christ, God the Father has promised to hear and answer whenever you call on his name.

Reflection and Discussion Questions

1. What qualities or characteristics does the name of "God the Father" evoke for you?

2. How can remembering that the Father is "in heaven" change how you pray? Does it humble you? Does it encourage you?

3. How can you strengthen your trust in the Father's care? (See Matt 6:32.)

4. Reflect on what the parable in Luke 10:11–32 instructs us about our nature as children, and God's nature as Father.

5. Is it reassuring for you to know that the Father understands your frame, "remembers that we are dust" (Ps 103:14)? Explain.

6. What does Jesus's prayer to the Father in Mark 14:36 teach you about praying?

CHAPTER 3

Glory to God

Hallow?

SOMETIMES WE USE A word whose meaning we don't really know. In our more sophisticated conversations, we like to drop references to "climate change" or "gender identity" just because everyone else does. But if someone asked us to define those terms, we'd be challenged to say exactly what we mean. The same problem afflicts the language of faith, where there are numerous words in common usage; they are mentioned in sermons, read in the Scriptures, and encountered in discussions at Bible study—words like "atonement," "covenant," and "sanctification." We employ this sanctified vocabulary, but beyond having a vague sense of what these words are about, we might not be able to say much.

One particular word in this category is something we say probably almost every day, even while we're doing the crucial activity of praying to God the Father. The word is "hallowed"—as in, "Our Father in heaven, hallowed be your name" (Matt 6:9). Do you know what are you doing when you "hallow" something? My dictionary tells me that "hallow" is a verb: "to make something holy; to honor something as holy." We can disregard the first definition, because Scripture reveals that God is holy already (Ps 99:3); he certainly doesn't need us to *make* his name holy. But to *honor* him as holy—that sounds more appropriate. As we begin our prayer to the Father through Jesus, we ask that God would be recognized for who he is, glorified as the holy Lord. For God is set apart in his glory, unique in his majesty and surpassing greatness—so much so that God is constantly praised by the angels in his heavenly throne-room as "holy, holy, holy" (Isa 6:3; Rev 4:8).

The Lord is the great God whom we are allowed to call upon in prayer and exalt in worship. And God says hallowing his name is our first and primary duty in life (1 Cor 10:31). "Glorify me in your prayers," the Lord says, "and glorify me in all that you do." This is the holy purpose that Jesus taught by echoing the worshipful spirit of the Psalms. In this chapter, we'll see how Jesus instructs us to hallow God's name in the first petition of the Lord's Prayer, and how God's name is hallowed in Psalm 29.

An Impressive Profile

When you meet certain people, they are quick to give you their business card. "Call me," they say, and on the card is all the contact information that you could ever want. And on that same business card—or maybe on their LinkedIn profile—are their official position and credentials. This fellow is a mortgage broker with a degree in finance. She's an appliance salesperson with fifteen years of experience, and has been a top producer six times. The point is, these people want you to see that they're qualified, that they are the ones you should call for a home loan or a dishwasher. It's a natural development: when you know someone's qualifications or credentials, this can inspire your confidence and can persuade you to turn to them for help.

This principle is similarly true in relation to God: knowledge inspires trust. We will be inspired to honor God's name, to trust him, and to seek his help when we see how impressive he is. Put negatively, you won't have much confidence in God if you don't know him. You probably will not turn to God for aid or encouragement if you don't have a sense of his character and his capability. Consequently, in the activity of hallowing of God's name, truly knowing him needs to be prior to anything else. This must be our boast, says Jeremiah—not in wisdom, strength, or riches, but in our knowledge of the Lord (9:23–24). Such an activity is not an optional exercise, for God has clearly revealed his great majesty (Rom 1:19–20). The Lord has left his "business card," if you will, and he has given us privileged access to his profile. And the reason we can know God well is because he speaks to us.

Words from Heaven

Mentioning God's speaking probably causes most of us to think of the Bible. After all, the Bible is called "the word"—it is the infallible expression of God's own mouth, words breathed out by his Holy Spirit and written down by the hand of human authors (2 Tim 3:16; 2 Pet 1:21). In the word, God speaks at length and unfolds many different facets of his glory for us to know and at which to marvel. But there is another testimony that God has given, another word he has spoken: the "word" of creation.

Probably most Christians are familiar with the opening words of Psalm 19, where David writes, "The heavens declare the glory of God, and the sky above proclaims his handiwork" (v. 1). There is a speech in progress whenever we walk outside, a continuous heavenly sermon concerning the majesty of the Lord: "Day to day pours out speech, and night to night reveals knowledge" (v. 2). The vast sky, the circling planets, the radiant stars and moon, and the brilliant sun—these all reveal the mighty God who created them. Through their sheer size and stunning beauty, the heavens are telling about God's power and wisdom. Their order and orbits are witnesses to the Lord's sovereignty over all and his faithfulness to what he created. The farther that mankind's vision is able to reach into the universe with high-powered telescopes and probes, the more we're staggered by God's grandeur. The heavens—indeed, all created things—bear the undeniable signature of their Creator. Everyone can see it, and everyone can hear it: "There is no speech nor language where their voice is not heard" (v. 3, NKJV). Whatever our language or literacy level, we can hear creation's song to its glorious Maker.

Psalm 19 celebrates how the holy God discloses himself both in the book of Scripture and the book of creation. And it's remarkable when we place these two books side by side, because with the one we can gain insight into the other. Scripture teaches us to go out under the night sky and consider the stars, or to bend down and admire the wildflowers. Go and listen carefully, watch closely, and stand humbly—because this great God, the one who created and upholds all things great and small, this magnificent God is also revealed in Scripture as our God and Father through Jesus Christ! And he wants us to hallow his name.

The Voice of the Lord

With that truth in mind, we listen to Psalm 29, for if anything resounds in this psalm, it is the "voice of the LORD." Fittingly, the one who wrote this psalm was a man of the outdoors. David, however, was not outside for leisure and recreation, camping for a couple weeks in the coziness of a tent or the security of an RV; he had to be outdoors on a regular basis, tending the flocks and herds of his father on the Judean hillsides (1 Sam 16:11). He was working, but several of his psalms suggest that David also had time to meditate on the eloquent words of the night sky, ample opportunity to listen to "the voice of the LORD."

It wasn't all peace and tranquility. When you think about the signature splendors of creation, you might picture a blazing sunset over the gently swelling waters of the ocean, or perhaps you envision noble mountain peaks, solid and reassuring. But when you are outside frequently and for extended periods of time, not by choice but by necessity, you encounter a darker side of creation. That beautiful sky can be shredded by a violent storm, a calm sea can suddenly grow angry and threatening, and you will see and feel how severe creation can be. Imagine David the young shepherd boy, hiding in the shelter of a rock as massive thunderclaps crash, the wind howls, and rain pelts down.

Such events were the most powerful forces known by the ancient peoples: violent thunderstorms, along with rattling earthquakes and the raging sea. Confronted with such spectacles, everyone trembled with fear. The potent tools of death and destruction today are automatic weapons and missile-laden drones; yet far more common on this earth, still terrifying and just as deadly, are the simple brute forces of God's creation: the earthquakes and volcanoes, the hurricanes and forest fires, the landslides and monsoons. Confronted with these things, we must still admit that we are powerless, that we can do little to defend ourselves or prevent damage or injury.

David might have been trembling in the storm, but he was also listening. For it's unmistakable: this is the voice of the Lord! It is God's voice "over the waters" (Ps 29:3) and within the rolling thunder (v. 3). It is the voice of the Lord "breaking the cedars," even smashing "the cedars of Lebanon" (v. 5). And it is his voice that "shakes the wilderness" (v. 8) and "strips the forests bare" (v. 9). Hear how it is simply God's voice that is accomplishing everything—a voice of great power! Like at the beginning of time, all that God needs to do is speak, and the world appears in obedience to his command (Ps 33:8).

God issues the word, and a massive typhoon creeps toward the Philippines. God speaks, and the earth under Mexico begins to rattle and roll. God orders from his holy throne, and a tsunami rises out of the Indian Ocean, bearing powerful witness to the truth of Psalm 29, "The voice of the LORD is powerful; the voice of the LORD is full of majesty" (v. 4). These are awesome displays of God's holiness—not the peaceful creation scenes that we love, but scenes of violence and destruction. Yet David gets the message loud and clear; he hears the resounding voice and understands that it is the Lord. This is God's heavenly glory as he shows his name to be hallowed in all the earth.

No Competition

Put together, God's intrinsic credentials form a long list: he has infinite power, flawless wisdom, unfailing goodness, perfect righteousness, steadfast mercy, and eternal truth. Next to this great

God, there is no competitor. This is how David begins in verse 1, throwing down a challenge to all the "heavenly beings" or the "mighty ones" (NKJV). He is probably referring to the gods of the surrounding nations, "the heavenly beings" that were reputed to do so much. In this first verse, David pictures God among the gods—something like a heavenly meeting room—with the Lord surrounded by Baal, Dagon, Asherah, Molech, and many others. These were the gods given the credit by ancient peoples for sending good weather, wealth, and military victory. The Canaanite god Baal was even known as the "Lord of thunder," for Baal was said to be the divine power animating every thunderstorm and bringing blessed rain.

But in the presence of the true God, all pretenders must bow and give him the glory. They must hallow his name! "Ascribe to the LORD, you heavenly beings, ascribe to the LORD glory and strength. Ascribe to the LORD the glory due his name; worship the LORD in the splendor of holiness" (vv. 1–2). David is rebuking these so-called mighty ones, highly vaunted by the nations: "Submit to God what is rightfully his! Confess that all glory and strength and honor belong to him alone!" You could say that the Lord is "stealing Baal's thunder," for Psalm 29 declares that the storms and rain and wind are the work of God alone. David sees that, in the truest sense, the Lord God is holy—he is set apart, without comparison or competitor in heaven or on earth.

God is unchanging, and so today God's voice goes out from his holy throne as it did before. His word is spoken and it is done. Today God still humbles the heroes of the world, shaming the false gods and ridiculing the empty idols. He can chastise peoples and their gods with tornadoes and cyclones, massive earthquakes, and fiery volcanoes. But God can also humble the nations with a financial crisis, civil unrest in the cities, or a new and virulent strain of disease. History demonstrates that it can happen so quickly that a mighty leader is brought low, an economy collapses, or a disaster strikes, leaving people gravely troubled and searching for hope—searching for him.

Through his marvelous works on earth, the Lord shows that he alone deserves the honor, and that this world's only stability is through his government. The sovereign God is reminding us that it is not presidents or prime ministers who get things done, and it is not the United Nations or the World Bank or Apple Inc. that will progress humanity. Our hope is not that some new technology will be able to create global harmony, or that the tolerant human spirit can deliver us from bloody conflict. In this age of idols, we need to hear Psalm 29 again as David urges us not to trust in the "mighty ones" and look to them for help, but to hallow God's name alone: "Ascribe to the LORD, you heavenly beings, ascribe to the LORD glory and strength."

Glory to God!

In the eleven short verses of Psalm 29, we find the name of God almost twenty times—it's all about the Lord. There is almost no room left for anyone else. That is how it should be, for God's voice will always overpower every other. Yet there is a human voice present here; it is so brief that you might overlook it. In the midst of all the rolling thunder, breaking cedars, quaking mountains, and shaking forests—in all the beautiful commotion of who God is and what God can do—his people respond. After all, a response is what the Lord wants; he left his card, described his credentials, and encouraged his people, "Call me."

And that's what they do in verse 9, even while another mighty forest is being demolished: "The voice of the LORD makes the deer give birth and strips the forests bare, and in his temple all cry, 'Glory!'" Imagine that cry going up from a crowd of worshipers in the temple courts at Jerusalem. Maybe you've heard an audience do this at a sporting event or a concert, when everyone shouts out with the same cheer—it can be impressive. This is what happens at the temple in Psalm 29 as everyone cries out to God in his terrible might and dominion, exclaiming as one person: "Glory!"

It is actually surprising that "Glory!" is all they say. After a violent thunderstorm passes over the house, or after watching a spectacular video of an erupting volcano in Hawaii, we might pull out every possible superlative: "That was absolutely crazy. The noise was incredible—I felt it in my chest. Those explosions were totally epic!" But the Psalm 29 worshipers know the liturgical truth revealed in Ecclesiastes 5:2, "God is in heaven and you are on earth. Therefore let your words be few." The worshipers are deeply humbled by God's majesty and the works of his hand. They know that human speech cannot capture it, that any earthly response is going to be inadequate. So they simply bow in his presence and declare God's singular greatness: "Glory!"

With that one word, they are performing their life's first duty, for they are hallowing God's name. They honor the Lord as holy, and they acknowledge that to him belongs all glory and strength, goodness and righteousness, mercy and truth. In his temple, they worship the Lord in the splendor of his holiness (Ps 96:9).

In the Storm

For David, for the temple worshipers—and for us—the mighty deeds of God should inspire humble and heartfelt praise. We know God as Lord and King and that his absolute and everlasting rule is carried out on our behalf. Though he is exalted in majesty, he still thinks of his little children; in all his self-sufficient and flawless glory, God the Father is committed to our salvation and devoted to our blessedness. We're so sure of this because he gave his word, and his word is truth (John 17:7).

This is the crowning comfort when so much in this world seems to be changing and uncertain. There are tempests, disasters, and famines. Not just on a global scale, and not just to the unfortunate people living in distant lands and developing countries—these are the kind of things that can befall us. Our lives can be distressed by poor health or financial hardship. There can be the misery of family conflict, or the pain of ridicule from unbelievers. For seasons of our life, it can feel like the very soil beneath our feet is shuddering, like merciless waves are thrashing our head. Even then, this is the voice of the Lord—this is God, issuing his good commands from heaven.

We might tremble with David while that storm continues to rage and the rain pelts down. We tremble, yet we rest safely in the shelter of the Rock, for we know it is our God directing all things. We know that just as suddenly as we were plunged into trouble, so quickly God can extract us; God merely has to speak, and we'll be saved. And even if he doesn't, and he doesn't bring us back to where we were before, our God is faithful. For Jesus's sake, God has promised to go with us, and he never breaks his word.

So just as David did, we have to learn to listen. We need to open our ears, listening to the voice of the Lord in creation and hearing his unmistakable voice in this world. We must listen, for God is telling us about himself, broadcasting through his works the truth about who he is as God. And we should also do some cross-referencing by holding the book of creation alongside the book of Scripture. Place the two beside each other and see that this awe-inspiring, wonder-working, miracle-performing God is *our* God. The glorious Lord of the universe is our Father, and the great King of kings is our Savior (1 Tim 6:15). The one who knows all the stars by name knows our names, too (Ps 147:4).

Becoming better acquainted with God's glory, we grow surer that he'll never forsake us. In the prayer of faith, we say: "O God, by myself I cannot do it. I'm weak and vulnerable. This situation is impossible for me, but all things are possible for you. You are great and mighty, and I rest in you alone." Faith means surrendering our human pride, relinquishing our need to solve and to manage and prognosticate, and embracing the invisible yet all-powerful triune God. When we trust God in the storms, we hallow his name and bring him delight.

Strength and Peace

Psalm 29 ends with an affirmation of God's steadfast love for his people. After listening in on the council of God among the gods, watching the weather patterns sweep across the globe, monitoring the currents of the seven seas, and hearing the tectonic plates collide beneath the earth, we zoom in. We see a very small nation, an insignificant people—it is the church, and God has not forgotten her. In his upholding of the entire universe, not once has God neglected the nation whom he chose for himself. She enjoys the great privilege of depending on his power, trusting in his wisdom, and finding refuge in his grace. For David writes this as the last word of his psalm: "May the LORD give strength to his people! May the LORD bless his people with peace!" (v. 11).

Notice the two gifts that God is requested to give to his people: strength and peace. It sounds simple, but it sums up everything we need. For our continued journey as holy pilgrims, for our ongoing labor as his servants, God will supply us with *strength* in body and spirit. And God will grant *peace* with himself through the forgiveness of all our sins. The Father shares his mighty strength through the Holy Spirit, and he works his unshakable peace through the Lord Jesus. He gives these gifts because we belong to him and are precious to him. With these two crucial gifts, we can hallow his name.

Soli Deo Gloria

So how do we echo Psalm 29? When we hear the voice of the Lord, we too, are called to make this confession: "Glory to God!" When we see the handiwork of God in this world and in our lives, we should hallow his name by giving him praise and honor. This is what Christ's people do whenever we come together on the Lord's day: we worship God through our songs, prayers, and gifts. But when we begin a new week of work and study and activity, those words ought to keep resounding: "Glory to God alone! Glory to God in everything that I do!" When we sincerely pray "Hallowed be your name," this should transform everything we do when we're not praying. After a prayer that God's name be hallowed, it is time to get to work with hallowing.

In this holy activity, Johann Sebastian Bach left us an example. He composed acres of music, and his compositions are

recognized as some of the most beautiful ever made. Among com-
posers, Bach's name is renowned, but he wasn't out for his own
glory. He was a devout Christian who sought to serve God through
his marvelous music. Like any artist, Johann signed his works. But
Bach had another signature too, one even more important than
his own name. When he finished writing a piece, he would often
write three letters: SDG. These three letters are the abbreviation
of a well-known Latin phrase: *Soli Deo Gloria*—to God alone be
the glory. Bach probably suspected that he would receive much
praise for his compositions, but he wanted to redirect all the compliments and acclaim to one place, to the God who saved him from
his sins and blessed him with life and ability. SDG declares that it's
not about you, it's about God!

Such is the spirit of Jesus's first petition: "Hallowed be your
name," a sure echo of the Psalm 29 prayer: "Glory to God!" On all
our works, we should inscribe SDG. Not just on our life's splen-
did accomplishments, not just on the things of which we're most
proud, but we should engrave SDG on everything we do—with our
hands, our mouth, our mind, our hammer, our sewing machine,
our computer—for all of it must be for the glory of God alone.

The first petition teaches that when we really know God,
our first concern will be bringing glory to his name. We should
do nothing to win the praise or compliments of other people. We
should do nothing out of custom or tradition, or just because it has
always been expected of us. May we not serve ourselves, and may
we shun this world's false gods who are endlessly demanding but
never satisfying. Instead, may all the glory be reserved for the one
true and living God: Father, Son, and Holy Spirit! Let us use all our
gifts for him, and submit every moment to him, so that we bring
glory to God and hallow his name.

Reflection and Discussion Questions

1. Where in creation do you see testimony to the glory and majesty of God? What does this reveal to you about him?

2. To glorify God, we must know God. In what way can a deeper knowledge of God lead us to worship him more enthusiastically and meaningfully?

3. Do you see a connection between the first petition, "Hallowed be your name," and the first commandment, "You shall have no other gods before me" (Exod 20:3)? Explain.

4. How does our affliction sometimes make it difficult to pray that God would receive the glory? How does our prosperity sometimes do the same?

5. What is the purpose of our life according to 1 Corinthians 10:31? How can this be put into practice in concrete ways?

6. Jesus prayed, "Father, glorify your name" (John 12:28). How did this simple prayer express the spirit of his life? What can we learn from his devotion to hallowing God's name?

CHAPTER 4

Bow before Christ the King

Failed States

IN THE LAST DECADES, the world has seen several "failed states," countries like Somalia, Afghanistan, and Haiti. These are countries where virtually everything has fallen apart, from the top of society right down to the bottom. In a typical failed state, the government is corrupt, poverty is widespread, and lawlessness thrives. You hear about these nations on the news as they lurch from one disaster to another, and as their citizens are caught up in an endless cycle of misery. The problem with these nations is not that no one is in charge; there is always a government of one form or another. For instance, there might be a dictator propped up by the military, or a prime minister "elected" unlawfully. Someone will always be giving direction to a country, for better or for worse. For as the leaders go, the people go. And if a government has no competence and integrity, the citizens will suffer.

This is similarly true for our own lives. Picture yourself for a moment as a country, albeit on a tiny scale. As a mini-nation, you have your natural resources and revenue, your defense mechanisms and alliances. And most importantly, there is someone in the governing position, someone who is effectively making the decisions and setting your course. So who directs where you go and how you live? Is ruling the kingdom *your* job? You and I would prefer this, for we all have an independent streak.

It has been this way since that dark day in Paradise when Adam and Eve rebelled against God's benevolent rule. Echoing our first parents, over the ages there have been countless people who said, "Never mind God, I am the king (or queen) around here. I'll make the decisions. I'll do as I please and then get the glory." It sounds like freedom, but it begins a perpetual cycle of dissatisfaction which so often ends in ruin. We like to seat ourselves on the throne and imagine that we have the wisdom and strength to handle things. But we don't. Even so, we're not doomed to fail forever—in Jesus Christ, we have a forgiving king. Repenting of our pride and seeking his grace, we bow before him, praying the second petition of the prayer he taught us: "Your kingdom come" (Matt 6:10). In answer, our loving king will show the way of victory, and not failure; the way of blessing, not curse.

Kingdom Confusion

Sometimes I wonder how the disciples first reacted when Jesus taught this petition: "Your kingdom come." Did they raise an eyebrow in confusion, or did they all nod in agreement, knowing exactly what he meant? I wonder, because Jesus said very little to explain his prayer.

As an aside, it is interesting that the only petition Jesus really commented on was the fifth, where we pray, "Forgive us our debts, as we also have forgiven our debtors." Right after teaching this prayer, Jesus added, "For if you forgive others their trespasses, your heavenly Father will also forgive you, but if you do not forgive others their trespasses, neither will your Father forgive your trespasses" (Matt 6:14–15). In a remarkable way, he underlined the importance of grace in this petition, insisting that we pardon the wrongs that other people have committed against us, just as God has forgiven our trespasses against him—about which we will say more in chapter 7. Jesus evidently understood our difficulty in forgiving someone else's sin, but for all the other petitions, including the "kingdom petition," Jesus offered no commentary.

And you might have expected Jesus to clarify this petition, for "kingdom" was a big idea at his time. Mentioning "kingdom" in the first century surely caused his countrymen to contemplate their present dismal situation, the land occupied for decades by the gentile invaders from the Roman empire. For many, the word "kingdom" evoked visions of hurtling the Roman legions into the Mediterranean and finally putting a son of David back onto the throne in Jerusalem. Jesus knew that his disciples were probably misinformed on this subject; even at his ascension into heaven, the disciples asked him, "Lord, will you at this time restore the kingdom to Israel?" (Acts 1:6). After three years of Jesus's teaching, they still thought that he had come to make Israel great again, to initiate some grand earthly kingdom.

God's Kingdom

From the first day of his public ministry, Jesus announced that the kingdom was on its way (Matt 4:17). Later, he told a series of parables about the unstoppable power and inescapable call of the kingdom (e.g., Matt 13:24–50). Jesus said that a new age was beginning in him, not an age of global military power or earthly maneuvering (John 18:36), but the time of God's long-awaited heavenly kingdom and his righteous rule (Matt 6:33). The disciples of Jesus ought to pray for *this* kingdom to come.

As with each part of the Lord's Prayer, Jesus's kingdom petition is a deep echo of Old Testament voices, particularly the Psalms. Old Testament Israel was God's kingdom, and the Lord himself was sitting on the throne—a glorious reality expressed, for instance, in the praise of Psalm 145:1: "I will extol you, my God and King, and bless your name forever and ever." While his kingdom is eternal and universal (Ps 145:13), God was pleased to work out its temporary and local administration through earthly representatives (Deut 17:14–20). The kings of Israel were men chosen by the Lord and placed on the throne to rule as he would rule, in justice and righteousness.

A quick review of Israel's kings from Saul to Jehoiachin reveals that some were godly and capable, but many were not—often with catastrophic results for Israel. A "failed state" is not a modern concept: wicked kings in Israel meant corrupt judges, false religion, famines and poverty, and a regular trouncing in war by the nations. This was not what God intended for his people; Israel needed a better king, a king who would rule in God's way and bless his nation. It is revealing that the anarchy and godlessness described in the book of Judges can be encapsulated in one verse: "In those days there was *no king* in Israel. Everyone did what was right in his own eyes" (Judg 21:25; emphasis added). Without a good and faithful king on the throne of Israel, the people of God were lost.

A Prayer for the King

Realizing their dire need for godly leadership, Israel prayed for a righteous king in Psalm 72. It is notable that this is one of a few psalms written by Solomon, the son and successor of David. Solomon was surely thinking of himself and his holy task when he prays in the opening verses, "Give the king your justice, O God, and your righteousness to the royal son! May he judge your people with righteousness, and your poor with justice!" (vv. 1–2). Solomon knew that if he was going to properly carry out the job of ruling as king, he would need God's indispensable gifts of righteousness and wisdom.

In his everlasting covenant with David, the Lord had promised that his line would continue and that one of his sons would always sit on Israel's throne (2 Sam 7:11–16). Psalm 72 is a prayer—and a prophecy—that each Davidic son will enjoy God's favor in the blessings of safety and protection, power and authority, endurance and honor. In David's line, there were certainly some distinguished sons, such as Solomon, Josiah, and Hezekiah. God blessed their leadership so that Israel experienced times of global influence, extraordinary prosperity, and stable peace. Yet the books of 1 and

2 Kings (retold in 1 and 2 Chronicles) tell the story of how each of these rulers was also dogged by sin and weakness.

In view of the inherent frailty of Israel's earthly kings, Psalm 72 is *by* Solomon and it is *about* Solomon, while it's also about someone greater. In this psalm, the people are praying for more than an earthly king. They expected one day to receive a king who would reign forever, a king to continue on the throne into perpetuity, for they pray: "May his name endure forever, his fame continue as long as the sun!" (v. 17). He would rule with perfect justice and establish enduring peace; as a king, he would give full and final release from all their enemies. "May this kingdom come," they prayed. And the prayer of Psalm 72 was answered—it was answered in Christ!

The Greater King

From the beginning of his life on earth, it was clear that Jesus was a king—just not the kind that most people expected. Before his birth, the angel heralded him as one of David's descendants when he announced: "The Lord God will give to him the throne of his father David, and he will reign over the house of Jacob forever, and of his kingdom there will be no end" (Luke 1:32–33). Then he was born in Bethlehem, David's royal city, and worshiped by the wise men as the "king of the Jews" (Matt 2:2). Though Jesus was a king, he grew up not in a prominent city, but in an out-of-the-way village (Matt 2:23), while as an adult he didn't even have a home (Matt 8:20). As for his appearance, "He had no form or majesty that we should look at him, and no beauty that we should desire him" (Isa 53:2).

When the time came to begin his greatest work, King Jesus entered Jerusalem riding on a humble donkey (Matt 21:7). For a little while, he wore a crown, but it was crudely fashioned from thorns (John 19:2). He was clothed with the purple of royalty, but it was borrowed (Mark 15:17). He held a scepter, but it was wooden, and then used to beat him on the head (Matt 27:29–30). On the cross, he was mocked with the ironic sign that was truer than anyone knew: "Jesus of Nazareth, King of the Jews"—and then he was killed by his own people (John 19:19).

The cross looked like the end, yet another disastrous kingship for Israel. But this was a king of a better kind, because where David and others failed, Jesus was completely faithful in his task. He was anointed with the Holy Spirit so that, in his life and suffering, he could do everything that God asked of him. Just three days after the shame of the cross, King Jesus rose from the dead in glory. Christ was resurrected, he ascended, and now he shares the Father's throne; as it says in Ephesians 1:20–21, "[God] seated him at his right hand in the heavenly places, far above all rule and authority and power and dominion." In heaven he lives and reigns, not as king of Israel, nor only of the church, but as king of all the world!

Prophesying in Psalm 72, Solomon cannot say enough about the king's glory and the blessings that he will bring to the nation: "May there be abundance of grain in the land; on the tops of the mountains may it wave; may its fruit be like Lebanon; and may people blossom in the cities like the grass of the field!" (v. 16). It's a picture of inestimable prosperity. These were tangible promises that spoke directly to the Israelites: when the barns were full of grain, the vineyards were laden with fruit, and the population was flourishing. Physical blessings meant God's indisputable favor on the king and his people.

The essential core of the Psalm 72 promise remains true today. We don't expect rich harvests and overflowing bank accounts, but much more: Christ lifts us out of spiritual poverty and lavishes on us the riches of his favor. The risen and ascended king rules all things in the universe, and his greatest priority is the salvation of his people. Continuing to speak about Christ's omnipotence in Ephesians 1, Paul says that God "put all things under his feet and gave him as head over all things to the church" (v. 22). The power held by the risen and exalted Christ is the power available to us! There is nothing too great for Christ to do, yet in his eyes no one is too small—though he is King of kings, he always has attention for his people. Psalm 72 says this about our king: "From oppression and violence he redeems their life, and precious is their blood in his sight" (v. 14). The king on the throne is patient and long-suffering. He sees our brokenness and he restores us. We know that the very blood in our veins is precious in his sight, for Christ the King was willing to pour out his own blood for us!

The Unfinished Petition

Despite the glorious and reassuring picture of Jesus's kingship, there is something unfinished in the second petition. Jesus teaches us to pray that the kingdom will "come," that it will keep advancing and eventually arrive in fullness. By his earthly ministry, and by his death, resurrection, and ascension, Christ brought God's kingdom very close, yet it is still in progress. He has made a good beginning, but his royal project is yet to be completed.

The expectation for a coming age of perfect peace and prosperity is heard in Psalm 72. The coming king is carrying with him immense blessing, but there are some trouble spots on the radar screen. Enemies are still circling, and the heat of battle can flare up at any moment, so the king's people are still in danger. In verse 4, where right next to all the considerate activities of the gracious king—doing justice, defending the afflicted, saving the needy—there is another essential work carried out by the Davidic sovereign: "May he defend the cause of the poor of the people, give deliverance to the children of the needy, and *crush the oppressor!*" Solomon and the people were praying for a gentle and loving king, and also a king who would be prepared to crush and destroy his enemies.

This royal Son will rule "from sea to sea," even to the ends of the earth as everything is subjugated to him (Ps 72:8–10). It is a grand and inspiring vision of total dominion. But how does the king acquire such a wide scope of power and establish total peace? By *conquest*—akin to how they say today: if you want peace, prepare for war! Solomon prophetically sees desert tribes and other enemies, kings of Tarshish and distant isles, arriving before the king (vv. 10–11). They're not coming to bring diplomatic greetings or to sign a free trade agreement, but they are coming in defeat.

They bow and give the king their gold and wealth as tribute; they even get down into the dust to show their submission. In Psalm 72, the people of Israel pray for the total victory of David's son, Jesush Christ: "May your kingdom come. May it come by dominating every other kingdom."

The people's urgent requests in Psalm 72 instruct us to pray the second petition in a more robust way than we might be accustomed to. As Jesus taught us, we do pray regularly that God's kingdom will grow through the preaching of the good news of Jesus in mission and evangelism (Matt 9:37–38). We also pray that God's kingdom will advance through needy people receiving relief in Christ's name, and through politicians promoting Biblically-sound legislation for our country's governance. These are unfinished prayers for the kingdom, and it is good to keep offering them to our king. But praying for God's kingdom to come means praying *all* of Psalm 72, even asking for the ruin of those who oppose our king. We should urgently plead that God's earthly enemies be crushed, that the devil's works be destroyed, and that his vile kingdom will collapse forever.

Praying for Victory

By his death and resurrection, Christ has already secured Satan's defeat and has guaranteed the victory of God. Satan is an enemy doomed to destruction, and he will surely lick the dust. But Christ's people must not complacently turn our backs, because there is still time for Satan to fight. Animals are most ferocious when they realize they are cornered and going to die—this is what Satan is like in his final days, enlisting any ally who can possibly damage God's kingdom. Prime ministers and CEOs, university professors and novelists, judges and lawmakers, entertainers and movie-makers, scientists, and even the theologians—so many join ranks with the prince of darkness. Together they conspire and launch their attacks against Christ and his word, against his kingdom and church (cf. Ps 2:1–3). Perhaps we are seeing this war of the two kingdoms more distinctly now than ever before. Today it is hard to ignore how the devil does everything he can to ruin God's works and to dilute Scripture's truth. In this war, he doesn't send out his little red men with forked tails and pitchforks—Satan is far subtler and much more dangerous.

The evil one directs his legions of followers: "Distract God's people from reading the Bible—make them so busy that they don't have time for it. Lure them with lust. Divide them with pride. Burden them with an excess of material things. Get them to believe that truth is relative. Divert them with constant entertainment. Lull them to sleep with false comforts. Confuse them with wrong teaching. Make them so undisturbed and so trouble-free that they grow lukewarm in prayer and love."

"And above all," Satan says, "get them to forget Jesus. Make the cross of Christ merely a fashion accessory, a background detail in their busy lives, something unimportant and forgotten." The deceiver wants us to forget Jesus because he knows that depending on him is the only way the church will persevere. If we are disciples who have lost touch with the Master, or if we are soldiers who don't know their king, we're probably not far from falling. So we must fix our eyes on Christ alone, and pray for victory: "O God, crush all your competitors—crush the idols of the nations, crush the gods in our hearts—and crush the devil once and for all, so that your kingdom may come in its fullness!"

And in answer to this petition, King Jesus is giving victories to his citizens. It is a victory when God's grace teaches us to say "no" to temptation, and when we take time to grow in the word. It is a victory when we can devote ourselves to building up his church, giving one donation at a time, training up one child at a time, worshiping one Lord's day at a time, offering one prayer at a time. These are small but significant building blocks in Christ's coming kingdom. We don't always appreciate small beginnings, but when we see such grace in our life and in the church, we should be assured that our king is on his throne and he is busy.

The start of God's good works constitutes a sure promise that he's going to bring them to a glorious finish (Ps 138:8). In the words of Psalm 72, the moment is near when "all kings [will] fall down before him, all nations serve him!" (v. 11). God's kingdom will come—it's a sure thing. Because Christ is the sovereign Lord, Satan's dark dominion will soon suffer its final defeat and the church will be fully gathered. The glorious day that is prophesied in Revelation 11 will soon dawn, when: "The kingdom of the world has become the kingdom of our Lord and of his Christ, and he shall reign forever and ever" (v. 15). His kingdom is coming, so let us ensure that we're praying for it and working for it. For if we are, our great king has promised that we will receive the crown of life (Jas 1:12; Rev 2:10).

Yielding to his Supremacy

If Christ the King is so glorious on his exalted throne and his victory so assured, what is the consequence? For citizens of his kingdom, there can be no hesitation. We must fall down on our faces and worship the king, yielding to his supremacy and surrendering to his greatness. This is one more aspect of our request in the second petition of the Lord's prayer, a request that we personally would be ruled and directed by Christ. The same spirit of submission fills Psalm 72, as Solomon and his people place themselves before their everlasting king: "May they fear you while the sun endures, and as long as the moon, throughout all generations" (v. 5). Revering him, they expect nothing from themselves, but grand things from the king alone.

It is still so difficult to submit. We want to make a declaration of our independence and be the ruler of our own little lives, seated on our own little throne over our own small kingdom. As King Reuben, I want to use my own strength and skill, trust alliances of my own making, and do whatever is right in my own eyes. This is why Jesus teaches you and me to keep praying, day after day, "Lord, may your kingdom come. May your rule of *my life* too, be total and constant. May you be the king of my weekend activities, and king of my quiet thoughts, king of my bank accounts and my daily work. May you be the king of my family, the king of my marriage, the king of my every relationship. Help me in all things to seek first your kingdom and your righteousness!"

Who's on the Throne?

Let's return to the beginning of this chapter. Picture yourself as a nation—a small territory, but important in God's eyes. In this land, who is king? In your life, who's in charge? Remember, there will always be someone directing your heart and guiding your life—for good or ill. So are you the commander-in-chief? Every self-governed life will end in failure, terrorized by guilt, spiritually bankrupt, and morally corrupt. Without repentance and faith, a person will even be counted among the enemies of Christ: licking the dust, bowing not in worship, but defeat. Or does the Lord rule your life, and do you look constantly to Christ sitting on the throne? Then you can count on his unchanging love, his inestimable blessing, and his stalwart protection, now and forever. Christ is the king who sacrificed his life for his people, a sacrifice by which he established "a kingdom that cannot be shaken" (Heb 12:28).

Knowing that King Jesus is on his throne, we earnestly pray: "May his name endure forever, his fame continue as long as the sun! May people be blessed in him, all nations call him blessed!" (Ps 72:17). Knowing King Jesus, we want to bow before his heavenly majesty, trust in his faithful care, submit to his steadfast word, and depend on his amazing grace. Then his blessing will rest upon us, now and forever, as we dwell in the kingdom of God and of Christ our Savior.

Reflection and Discussion Questions

1. How do you sometimes attempt self-rule? What have been the results for your life?

2. How does Christ's total and enduring kingship over this world give you a sure comfort?

3. Christ is King, but Satan is called "the ruler of this world" (John 12:31). Where do you experience the reality of kingdoms in conflict?

4. How does Christ's kingship call us to action as those who are citizens of his heavenly kingdom (Phil 3:20)?

5. The second petition, "Your kingdom come," is forward-looking to when "the kingdom of the world has become the kingdom of our Lord and of his Christ, and he shall reign forever and ever" (Rev 11:15). Do you pray for Christ's return? How does this expectation change how you live (see 2 Pet 3:11–13)?

CHAPTER 5

Teach Me Your Paths

Highways and Byways

HAVE YOU RECENTLY BEEN lost? Toiled to get from Point A to Point B? I doubt it, because today it is pretty straightforward to find your way around. Plenty of help with navigating is available: you can go to Google Maps and find precise directions to the destination of your choice, or you can be guided everywhere by an app on your phone. Even in foreign cities or places you've never visited, it is difficult to get lost if you have the right tools. If only the rest of life was as simple to navigate—if only it was always uncomplicated finding our way to good decisions! I'm not only referring to life's notable and weighty choices, for we all understand that deciding on a career, choosing a potential wife or husband, or making a significant purchase like a vehicle or house can be an arduous process. Such choices are the significant highways that we decide to take, setting out in a direction we might follow for years—even for the rest of our life.

But besides these big decisions, each day we have a multi-tude of lesser choices to make. These are the countless avenues and side-streets along the way, the small decisions about what we're going to say to our spouse about the towel on the bathroom floor (again), or what attitude to take toward an unexpected bill from the mechanic. These are the fleeting decisions about what we're going to do with this hour of free time before dinner, or how much effort to apply to our homework or our housework. Such scenarios might seem comparatively trivial, but finding the right way isn't effortless. Our heart still inclines in the wrong direction, and we are easily sidetracked. We should be constantly attentive to the route we're on, yet we so readily turn on cruise control and stop thinking about what God our Father wants us to do.

With good reason then, Jesus teaches us to pray in the third petition of his prayer: "Your will be done, on earth as it is in heaven" (Matt 6:10). He wants us to pray on a daily basis: "Lord, may my entire life be directed by you. In things major and minor and middling, please teach me what pleases you. My Father in heaven, may your way be the way that I willingly follow always." As we have been learning throughout this book, the third petition is also a clear echo of the Psalms—particularly of David's prayer in Psalm 25. In this psalm, a humble child of God prays to receive a reliable spiritual compass; he asks for instruction in God's will, together with the strength and submissiveness to put it into practice. It is a daily prayer for each of us as we navigate life's highways and byways.

Arguing with the Navigator

If you've ever had the experience of getting lost with a companion, you will know that it is easy to start arguing. The driver gets annoyed with the navigator for instructions that are less than helpful. But the navigator thinks she has been quite clear, considering that she is relaying directions straight from the GPS—it's the driver who is not reacting fast enough. The frustration quickly mounts, turning irritation into anger.

An argument is also at the heart of our struggles with doing God's will, for there is often a difference of opinion about directions: I think that I should go one way, and God says that I should go another. And it's not that one route is more scenic, the other more direct; it is a difference with consequences. Frequently we want to take our own way because we believe that it's actually better for us, while God says that taking our own way can be fatal. It's a highway to nowhere, and it could even turn into a dead end. But we disagree and dispute with the navigator.

This kind of inner argument happens more often than you might think. For instance, you want to watch the television series that everyone is talking about, but you hear that each episode has at least one graphic sex scene. You're aware of God's view on things like this, yet you have your own preference—so what do you do? Or you realize that your next-door neighbor needs help, or that you should show hospitality to a new family at church, but it will probably be awkward and consume some of your precious leisure time. What to do? Or maybe you would like to stay at this great party for an hour or two more, but it means you probably won't be effective tomorrow at work, or you won't be attentive in worship. What do you do?

Life can be complex, but in countless situations, the options are actually quite simple. If we reflect, we start to comprehend what it's really about: "Am I going to do what I want here? Will I have tunnel vision, and pursue my own enjoyment and comfort? Or will I do what is right? Will I listen to what God says in Scripture, and what his Holy Spirit has taught me by experience?" Even some of our smallest decisions can be condensed into these opposing directions: "Will I be turning right or left? Doing good or evil? Will I be listening to God or to someone else?"

And the enticement to take our own way is constant. The Bible says that this is the way that our hearts incline (Ps 141:4). Compare it to when the wheels on a car are out of alignment after clobbering a curb—now the vehicle stubbornly pulls in one direction, and the driver needs to resist it constantly. In the same way, we incline to sin: pulling toward disobedience, pulling away from God. Such is our struggle when praying "your will be done." For we already have our own idea of what we want to do. We need to pray, "Lord, may your will be done," even when it feels like every cell in our body wants to give in to this temptation. The reality is that our decisions are often wholly propelled by emotion or desire, and it's only later that we might look for a few "good" reasons to support our wrong choice and to justify our sin. Self-denial is not a virtue that comes naturally. We don't seek God's wisdom first; instead, we tend to rely on our own understanding (Prov 3:5). We argue with the navigator—or just don't listen to him—even as we get more and more lost.

Humble Enough to Ask

David's struggle to know and to do God's will is heard throughout his prayer in Psalm 25. He begins by looking to God: "To you, O LORD, I lift up my soul. O my God, in you I trust" (vv. 1–2). He is committing his direction to God, resolving to listen to his instruction. In a similar spirit, we might resolve to do that at the beginning of a new day: "Lord, today I really want to serve you." But it's not easy. As Psalm 25 demonstrates, almost immediately there is trouble brewing and sin looming, for David goes on to say: "Let me not be put to shame; let not my enemies exult over me" (v. 2).

This is another psalm for which we don't know David's precise situation, but it sounds like enemies were trying to discredit him. He was probably king at this time, and traitorous foes were bullying him and besmirching his good name. By making accusations, they were trying to incite a violent reaction. They hoped that everyone would see then what kind of nasty person David really was, that he couldn't be trusted and shouldn't be king. This was a tight spot for David. If he does nothing, his enemies will get the last word and probably turn people against him. But if he reacts to their slander, it's likely that they'll just get more ammunition to fire at him. It's a tough quandary, so in this psalm, David urgently prays for God's guidance (vv. 4–5). He needs to navigate this minefield without blowing himself up!

At the same time, David prays that he will not sin. In the past, he had sometimes reacted harshly to his enemies—or had nearly done so—and there were certainly times when he depended on his own wisdom instead of being led by God. This awareness of weakness is probably the reason that he includes a confession of sin in his prayer for guidance: "Remember not the sins of my youth or

my transgressions; according to your steadfast love remember me"
(v. 7). It takes a lot of humility to say that when you're requesting
help!

I am probably not the only one who hates to ask for directions—even if I'm just looking for the correct aisle in the grocery
store—because I like to pretend that I have most things figured
out. But when looking for the path to a good decision, we should
acknowledge before God our total need. We ought to pray, "Father,
help me not take my own way, like I did last time. In the moment
of deciding, in the moment of reacting, help me not to be so stubborn and selfish. My paths have always been sinful, and my decisions always poor. That is why I need your guidance—and your
forgiveness—so badly." And as a gracious Father, he will answer us
in his faithfulness.

Hard Questions

When we are confronted with another of life's myriad choices, it is
sometimes very obvious what we must *not* do. Should I stay home
from the worship service on Sunday morning? No, I should go.
Should I lie to my parents about what happened today at school?
No, I ought to tell them. Should I share this juicy morsel of gossip?
No, the story needs to end with me. We all know God's "big rules"
about right and wrong (Exod 20:1–17). We don't always listen to
them, but we do *know* them!

But besides the areas of life that are clearly ordered by God's
commandments and the other injunctions of Scripture, how do I
find my way? How can I learn God's will more specifically? In the
particular place where God has put me, what is most pleasing to
him? That isn't always so clear. For instance, there can be the com-
plicated challenge of relationships in your family when some are
nonbelievers, or when there has been an ugly conflict in years past.
There is the thorny matter of how to interact with a hostile and
unbelieving world, the people who don't always treat us fairly but
who still need to hear the gospel of Christ. Or if you have your own
business, there can be hard questions about debt, profit margins,

and environmental responsibility. In the intricacies of daily life, there is not always a sharp line between calling something good and calling something evil (Rom 14:1–23). The fact is, Scripture doesn't speak with an unmistakable voice on every possible situation that we will face.

Enough Light

Because of life's ambiguity and complexity, we wish sometimes that God would speak audibly and directly about what is pleasing to him. Then we could be like the angels alluded to by Jesus in this petition, those holy servants receiving God's directives and "doing his will in heaven" so willingly and faithfully (Ps 103:20–21). Getting messages straight from the Lord on his heavenly throne would be simple: "Reuben, I want you to do this. Go there tomorrow with this message. This is the decision you should make." That's divine instruction to which we could happily submit—but would we? Or perhaps we wish that God would give a detailed map for our life, something like following the gentle promptings of your GPS: "In three hundred meters, turn right. Make a U-turn when possible."

Yet this won't happen, for the excellent reason that God wants us to trust in him. We prefer to have everything sorted out and our lives planned in five or ten-year increments. But God's direction is often given merely from day to day. He might shine only enough light to show the next small step that we need to take (Ps 119:105)—the next opportunity, the next duty—and nothing more.

In this regard, the Father's daily provision of guidance is comparable to the petition about our bread which we'll study in the next chapter. When it comes to our bodily needs, God promises to give enough food and drink to sustain us, one day at a time (1 Tim 6:8). We might have access to much more than this, but his promise is for *today*. The same is true for our knowledge of God's will, for he often gives immediate instruction, a daily directive, and nothing more: "This is your assignment for today. Don't worry about next month, or what you have to do next year. This is

my will for what you need to do, right now." God does this because
he is teaching us not to forecast and fret about the future. Surely
God our Father is also preventing us from getting too comfortable,
from starting to coast carelessly because we know exactly what the
road ahead is like.

Most importantly, God wants us to keep returning to him in
prayer for wisdom and direction. He wants us to be dependent on
his guidance, each new day: "Father, what's the next thing? In this
new day, with its many opportunities and varied challenges, show
me how I can serve you faithfully, so that your will is done." As
James exhorts, "If any of you lacks wisdom, let him ask God, who
gives generously to all without reproach, and it will be given him"
(1:5). We might be conflicted and confused, but when asking God
for wisdom, we can be confident that he'll answer, like David was
confident in Psalm 25. He was in a tight spot, and could've de-
spaired and given up, or done the first (sinful) thing that came
to his mind. But recall how he begins with a confession of faith:
"O my God, in you I trust" (v. 2). Before he says anything else,
before he mentions his perplexity or his inclination to sin, David
confesses that God will never abandon those who belong to him.
This is the powerful way to begin our daily prayer for direction: "O
my God, in you I trust."

Lead Me in Your Truth

In the same trusting spirit, David prays his marvelous prayer to
know God's will: "Make me to know your ways, O LORD; teach
me your paths. Lead me in your truth and teach me, for you are the
God of my salvation; for you I wait all the day long" (vv. 4–5). Notice that David doesn't ask to see a heavenly sign, or to hear a quiet
whisper in the night. Rather, he asks for knowledge, teaching, and
meaningful insight into God's word. Whenever Scripture speaks
of God's "ways" like David does here, it is referring to the ways of
his covenant law (Deut 10:12; Josh 22:5). And whenever Scripture
speaks of God's "paths," it is describing those routes for life that
are traced out in the word (Ps 119:35). In his present uncertainty

David asks to see—or to remember—the abiding truths of Scripture that he needs to act on: "Show me these ways." Scripture is where he expects to learn God's will in this demanding situation.

We pray Psalm 25 with David: "Father, teach me your paths." The verb "teach" is well-chosen, because it implies that we need to learn. Whether at school or taking up a new skill in the workshop, all learning takes attention and exertion. So it is with God's will: it requires study to learn what pleases God in the countless moments of life. And if we want to find God's will, we should look in Scripture, the place where thousands upon thousands of his words are written down for our "training in righteousness" (2 Tim 3:16).

When we saturate our minds with the Lord's word, we begin to think in the Lord's ways (Rom 12:1–2). Our bad alignment is being corrected, and we're becoming increasingly oriented toward God and his purposes. As our minds and instincts are gradually shaped by Scripture, we learn more of God's will, until we can start to say, "*This* is what God wants—he told me in his word. I know that he wants me to dismiss these bitter thoughts. I know that he wants me to use my gifts with excellence. He wants me to be faithful to my wife, serve my family, and contribute to Christ's church. In the end, this is not a hard decision, because I know that God always wants me to put him first. And I pray that his will may be done."

Training in the word is something we must do in advance. In the moment of making a decision or settling on a course of action, we don't always have time to contemplate questions of right and wrong. Life is dynamic and quickly hurries onwards. It's like merging onto the freeway when we only have seconds to decide: accelerate or slow down, move to the left or stay on the right. In situations like this, we rely on our instincts which are (hopefully) finely-tuned by experience. And this is when our need for godly wisdom is most apparent. Even when having an ordinary conversation, or starting a small project at work, or sitting down at the table for breakfast, there are immediate questions of how we are going to act and whose will we are going to do. What is God's will for my words to this careworn person? What is God's will for these boring labors in the office? What is God's will about the tension in my marriage these days? The demands are immediate, and we are just seconds away from sinning. So we ask God to keep teaching us. May he get us out of our self-satisfied rut, eliminate our blind spots, and hone our instincts. Humbly acknowledge to God that what you want doesn't matter, and then search the Scriptures to learn what God wants, asking for a spirit of strength and submission to put it into practice.

He Will Confide

To find God's will requires becoming attuned to his leading. For God nudges and prods us, opens some doors and closes others. We should pay attention to these things, and we do so by living in close fellowship with the Lord; as David confesses in Psalm 25, "Who is the man who fears the LORD? Him will he instruct in the way that he should choose" (v. 12). A heart reverent before the Lord is a teachable heart. Building on that confession is David's profound revelation a couple verses later: "The LORD confides in those who fear him; he makes his covenant known to them" (v. 14, NIV). When we love and honor God in all his greatness, when our eyes are daily fixed on him, he takes us into his confidence and shares his wisdom for our lives.

Compare it to the openness and mutual understanding that are enjoyed between two close friends. If we only rarely spend time with a person, we're not really going to identify with him or share anything meaningful. But if we see each other a lot, the words start to flow. We find out each other's views, desires and aversions, even secrets—and a friendship grows. In the same way, when we live in covenantal friendship with the Lord—when we commune with him through prayer and listen to his voice in the word—he shows us what to do. He works within us a penetrating knowledge of his will and he shares his intimate counsel. When we walk with God, he confides in us about what is right and pleasing to him, and he also encourages us to do it.

God teaches us his will through his word, but he also teaches us through the people whom he has positioned around and beside us. We're blessed to have communion with fellow believers, so we should be prepared to listen to parents, godly friends, wise teachers, and church leaders, those people whom we know have been given the Holy Spirit. If we are humble enough to seek advice and ask for guidance, we can receive much good insight from the Lord.

He Will Guide

Even so, the struggle can remain. After many days of searching humbly and prayerfully for God's will, we can still be completely unclear about what he wants us to do. This is perplexing and discouraging, but in our days of waiting, Jesus teaches us to keep praying the Psalm 25 petition: "Make me to know your ways, O LORD; teach me your paths. Lead me in your truth and teach me" (vv. 4–5). We can pray this with assurance, knowing that God will surely answer his children as he has promised.

Listen to what David confesses in the midst of his puzzlement: "Good and upright is the LORD; therefore he instructs sinners in the way. He leads the humble in what is right, and teaches the humble his way" (vv. 8–9). Underline the hinge in that passage, the "therefore." *Because* God is upright, he will instruct us in his ways. *Because* God is good, he will surely guide us in what is right. Like every petition of the Lord's prayer, "your will be done" is rooted in God's character of steadfast love. He will lead and enable us in doing his will, for this is who the Father is: he is faithful to all who call on his name in Christ.

It is good to remember that even the one who taught the third petition needed the Father's guidance. When he was a youth, Jesus had to grow in wisdom (Luke 2:40), and later he required the Holy Spirit's special anointing so that he could submit to the Father's will during his ministry (Luke 3:22). This learning continued throughout his life and culminated with his dying for sinners; as Hebrews says about Jesus, "Although he was a son, *he learned obedience* through what he suffered" (5:8). Now that Christ has been "made perfect" (Heb 5:9), he sends us the gift of his Spirit so that "we have the mind of Christ" (1 Cor 2:16). When we have the mind of Christ, we learn to apply his way of thinking to every situation that we face. We learn to love humble service in our homes and our communities because Christ became a servant. We start to love our enemies because we know that Christ loved his. We seek God's glory in all that we do because that is what Christ always did. He not only taught us to pray "Your will be done," he also embodied this prayer in his life and death (Matt 26:39–42).

Putting it into Drive

After all this, there remains an enormous difference between knowing what road to take and actually following it. If we enter a destination into our phone or GPS, but then stay parked in our driveway, the only thing that will change is our estimated time of arrival. This is why the third petition has an emphasis on action: more than knowing God's will, we must *obey* it. During the same sermon in which he taught the Lord's Prayer, Jesus warned, "Not everyone who says to me, 'Lord, Lord,' will enter the kingdom of heaven, but the one who does the will of my Father who is in heaven" (Matt 7:21). Even when we study God's word and become convicted of what he wants us to do, there is often still a struggle. This is because doing God's will is the harder way, or we fear the consequences, or it's just not what we feel like doing right now. We hesitate, but Jesus encourages us to take ourselves out of "Park" and get into gear.

We can accept God's guiding and listen to his leading, and then go forward in the knowledge that the Father will bless our obedience. As David pondered the present crossroads, he held onto this confession: "All the paths of the LORD are steadfast love and faithfulness, for those who keep his covenant and his testimonies" (Ps 25:10). He is saying that God shows love to the obedient, that God is faithful to the faithful. Though we owe the Lord every bit of our allegiance and service (and infinitely more), he rewards us in his grace, blessing the doers of his word.

In this petition, Christ exhorts us to press on and perform God's will. We still have our questions about what pleases him—in this life, such uncertainties will never disappear—but we do know that our chief purpose is to bring glory to God and to his Son, our Savior (1 Cor 10:31). Like the holy angels in heaven, we are here on earth to serve our God, gladly and loyally. Directed by his word and filled with his Holy Spirit, we have unchanging coordinates by which we may always travel. If we ask, the Father will help us to live this petition: "Make me to know your ways, O LORD; teach me your paths. Lead me in your truth and teach me, for you are the God of my salvation."

Reflection and Discussion Questions

1. When making daily decisions, do you ever experience the tension of "inner arguments" as described in this chapter? What is typically the outcome?

2. Jesus warns against making an outward confession of God, but not doing his will (Matt 7:21). Why is this such a serious danger for us?

3. In what areas of your life presently do you see a particular need for wisdom to know God's will? How are you seeking his direction?

4. How does Christ's promise in John 16:13 encourage you when praying "your will be done"?

5. David is sure that "the LORD confides in those who fear him" (Ps 25:14, NIV). Think about a time when you have experienced this to be true.

6. In what way is Christ the perfect example of someone who prayed and embodied the third petition? (see Matt 26:39–42) What can we learn from the pattern of his life?

CHAPTER 6

The Fountain of Blessing

Revealing Praise

WE PRAISE GOD FOR what we most value. If something is important to us, it will probably ascend to the top of any praise in our prayers to God. We studied hard, so we praise the Lord for good marks on our exams. We've been sick, so we thank God for improved health. We praise God for our children, our friends, for work, or a time of vacation. And we *should* do this—it is right to praise and thank God for his many gifts. The Psalms are the ultimate example of such praise, demonstrating that God's people will never run out of reasons to worship him. As Psalm 146:2 says, "I will praise the LORD as long as I live; I will sing praises to my God while I have my being." Truly, there is always another cause and motive to rejoice in the Lord our God!

On the subject of reasons for praise, in this chapter we reflect on the gift of our daily bread. The fourth petition of the Lord's Prayer is about how God the Father promises to provide for all our bodily needs: "Give us this day our daily bread" (Matt 6:11). Food and drink, housing and clothing, health and breath are blessings for which we need to petition God each day—and when we receive them, we should thank and praise the Lord.

Psalm 65 is an instructive example of this gratitude, for here David and the Israelites praise God for sending rain on the land and providing a rich harvest. They are exuberant in worship, even for what seems like a simple gift. This psalm sets a revealing mirror in front of us; it asks whether we too, praise God for our daily bread and worship him for his generosity. Are we still moved to humble gratitude by God's basic material gifts? Or do we focus on blessings that seem more interesting, more novel—more important? Sincerely praising God for his gifts is hard when we're accustomed to having a lot. Relying on God to provide seems unnecessary when it feels like there is absolutely no uncertainty about tomorrow's food supply. If we know about wealth, and we're not-so-dependent anymore on the Father to support us, Psalm-65-style praise isn't going to flow freely from us. But in echoing this psalm in the fourth petition of his prayer, Jesus teaches us to praise and trust our Father for his never-failing stream of blessing.

Acknowledge the Giver

When our youngest daughter received a pair of walkie-talkies for her birthday last year, I learned again the importance of *acknowledging*. When you are communicating via walkie-talkie, the person on the other end needs to know that you're there, and that you've heard them: "Copy that," you say. In a similar way, at the heart of true prayer is the simple activity of acknowledging. When we talk to God sincerely, we're not ignoring him. By speaking with God every day, we are showing that he is important to us, confessing that we need his help, and rejoicing that he is near. And particularly when we pray for our daily bread, we are letting the Father know that our eyes are open for his glory and generosity.

It may seem an obvious point, but it is difficult to thank someone for a gift if you don't know who gave it you. Our family once came home from an outing and discovered a present at our front door. It was a thoughtful and generous gift, but there was no card or message with it—no "To," no "From," just a wrapped present. It sort of bothered us that we didn't know where the mystery gift came from, and we tried to figure it out, because we really wanted to say thank you. To acknowledge a gift, you need to know the giver. I said it was obvious, but we have the tendency to overlook the obvious. And because of that, we sometimes forget that everything we have is from the open hand of the Father. From a human perspective, we ourselves furnished what we needed. Our hard work, or superior ability, or careful budgeting, or wise investing should be given the credit for our current status or success. But actually, all of it came from God—the labors and their results—and we should humbly speak to him to acknowledge this.

Singing a Harvest Hymn

This grateful acknowledgement is on display in Psalm 65. Commentators have called it "a harvest hymn" because David may have composed it for the beginning of the annual harvest in Israel. As the people were heading out to the fields to bring in the wheat and barley, the grapes and olives, they happily acknowledged God the Lord as the source of every blessing with this song, "You crown the year with your bounty, and your carts overflow with abundance" (v. 11, NIV).

It might have been a song for harvest, but another possibility is that Psalm 65 was written as a song of thanksgiving when a drought or famine had come to an end. In verse 3, there is an aspect of confession of sin—"When we were overwhelmed by sins, you forgave our transgressions" (NIV)—so perhaps God had recently been disciplining his sinful people with drought (Deut 28:23–24). But now it's over: sin has been forgiven, rain has begun to fall once more, and the fields are showing the promise of a fine harvest. In any case, the prosperity being celebrated in Psalm 65 is something for which the Israelites had prayed to God: "O you who hear prayer, to you shall all flesh come" (v. 2). Even though they had sinned previously, perhaps by depending on the false gods of the nations, now they remember where to look. In their need, they go to the Lord God who hears prayer, knowing that he will surely answer.

They express their grateful recognition of the Lord in verse 4: "Blessed is the one you choose and bring near, to dwell in your courts! We shall be satisfied with the goodness of your house, the holiness of your temple!" David describes God's temple as being a depository of blessing, like a warehouse packed to the rafters with good gifts. The rains that fell from the sky, the flourishing crops, the thriving flocks—it all came from the temple. It didn't literally originate from the Jerusalem temple (or tabernacle), of course, but the glorious presence of God was the source of all the goodness that Israel received. It was the Lord who was richly satisfying his people.

Come to the Fountain

David portrays the blessing from God in a striking way, for the Lord is pictured as a gardener busy tending his flowers and working his veggie patch: "You visit the earth and water it; you greatly enrich it" (Ps 65:9). The image of God "visiting the earth" conveys the sense of God coming near and "dropping in." In other passages of Scripture, God visits the earth in order to judge sinners (Isa 23:17), but here God comes close to show his goodness and impart a blessing! He visits the earth and waters it, like we might do in our garden on a summer morning, giving water to every plant that needs it.

As his praise builds, David emphasizes the gift of water: "The river of God is full of water; you provide their grain, for so you have prepared it. You water its furrows abundantly, settling its ridges, softening it with showers, and blessing its growth" (vv. 9–10). We often complain about the rain, but David has an enthusiastic appreciation for precipitation. Israel was a dry and arid land which received rainfall only at certain times of the year. There could even be years when the rains didn't come at all and almost every living thing suffered. Consequently, new sources of water were always being sought, and when they were found, wells and cisterns were built. Life could not survive without adequate water, but with a good and steady supply, life was preserved and able to thrive. Psalm 65 is a beautiful depiction of God's loving care for the earth, as he tends his garden, watering its furrows and softening it with showers. After another long and hot summer, it was a great gift when the Lord poured refreshing rains down onto the land. The hard clods of earth are broken up, David says, and the earth is moistened, so seeds can penetrate, germinate and proliferate. There will be a harvest because God gives the water!

In all this goodness, God is like a fountain. Picture a fountain that you might see in a city park, where there is a constant stream of water, gushing up and shooting out. That is what God is like: an endless flow of blessing, the fountain of all good! We find the same imagery in Psalm 36 where David says, "They feast on the abundance of your house, and you give them drink from the river of your delights" (v. 8). To his thirsty people God promises that we can kneel at his river and be satisfied, for the gracious Lord is like a gushing source of water: "With you is the fountain of life" (Ps 36:9). God's life-giving waters feed the streams and rivers, supply the clouds, refresh the land, nourish the crops, and quench our thirst. Every drop is sourced from the fountain in heaven above!

Without God's water, we would be lost. Without the simple gift of water, we would have no food on our tables and nothing to drink in our cups—and without this water, we would die, every one of us, in probably less than a week. But God sends water so that life can continue. That is the result of God's rainfall in the closing verses of Psalm 65: "You crown the year with your bounty, and your carts overflow with abundance" (v. 11, NIV). God sends the rains, gives growth in the fields and pastures, and enables the people's work, with the result that there is much blessing in the land. A good harvest is no accident—this is something God has done.

A Joy-filled Response

Those who receive the Lord's gracious nurture and steadfast care must respond in a fitting way. Listen to Psalm 65:12: "The pastures of the wilderness overflow, the hills gird themselves with joy." And verse 13: "The meadows clothe themselves with flocks, the valleys deck themselves with grain, they shout and sing together for joy." David says that creation itself rejoices in the generous provision of God. When you go for a walk, sometimes you can virtually hear creation sing. If there has been a recent rainfall, the colors of the flowers appear suddenly brighter, the grasses and leaves are refreshed, and everywhere there are birds and insects—it's a symphony of praise in color and sound for God the Creator! That is what the Israelites also witnessed when they went out to the fields for harvest: a worship-filled testimony to the only fountain of all good.

This teaches us that if the little hills rejoice and the valleys shout for joy and sing—if even the trees of the field clap their hands—our answer to the Lord should be no less genuine and enthusiastic. Do we, God's own children, remember to acknowledge our Father as the gracious Giver? We see the gifts and know who has given them: "Every good gift and every perfect gift is from above, coming down from the Father of lights with whom there is no variation or shadow due to change" (Jas 1:17). So we should praise him and give thanks with a joyful heart! This is what David confesses at the outset of Psalm 65, "Praise is due to you, O God" (v. 1). As our generous and giving Lord, God is most worthy of our grateful prayers, songs, and worship.

Remember and Ask

The trouble is that our appreciation for God's mercies quickly fades, and our gratitude is soon forgotten. When we are accustomed to having plenty, we said, it feels unnecessary to acknowledge God for the little stuff. It's disconcerting how quickly we can push God to the fringes of our mind. Did we truly thank him today? Did we ask for his blessing on our working and studying and planning? Instead of being grateful, we sometimes wish that we had more than this, better than this. No sooner has a blessing been received than we find something wrong with it: we wish our security was a little more secure, our happiness a little happier. The petition for our daily bread corrects us with Jesus's reminder that everything we have comes from the Father. If God gives a surplus, we certainly ought to praise him, but we must remember to praise and thank him for the basics, too.

This lesson is reflected in what Paul writes: "If we have food and clothing, with these we will be content" (1 Tim 6:8). Such teaching makes the fourth petition a bold yet modest prayer. Modest, because we should not bring God a wish list as long as our arm, even if we can easily compile a dozen petitions for a range of comforts and luxuries. But the fourth petition is also bold, for Jesus allows us to ask the Father for all of life's basic necessities. We ought to reflect on what we physically require for serving God and following Christ. God calls me to a life of faith and obedience—so do I have life? Do I have breath in my lungs? Do I have strength in my hands and clarity of mind? Do I have food in my stomach? Am I able to get up this morning and do what God has called me to do? For these things I will confidently ask my Father.

A Petition of Expectation

If you were cynical, you might ask David to turn down the volume of Psalm 65—the only reason joy abounds in Israel is because the harvest was so substantial! Anyone can praise God when the earth is dripping with abundance and the barns are overflowing. Translating this to our time, we can say that anyone will have a thankful feeling when revenue jumps by 20 percent. We would be pretty hard-hearted not to feel grateful when we just received an increase in our wages. It is almost natural to feel thankful in times of plenty—so maybe Psalm 65 isn't such a great example of gratitude. Because what about when there is a drought, a slowdown in the economy, layoffs at the factory, or a debilitating illness making someone unable to work? Can we still praise God if our accounts aren't brimming with wealth? We can! When the Lord gives a harvest in the field, at the factory, or in the office, we ought to sing this psalm. But that isn't the only time, for we should also sing this psalm and pray this petition in expectation. Jesus instructs us to anticipate the good gifts of God and to count on his promise, even in lean times and days of scarcity.

A spirit of expectation also fills Psalm 65, for it is not just a harvest party in the present, but a prayer for the future. We know this from what David says in verse 5: "By awesome deeds you answer us with righteousness, O God of our salvation." Whenever the Bible speaks about God's righteousness, we are being assured of God's character as the reliable one; he unfailingly keeps his word and always upholds his promise. There is hope in what God is yet to do: he will answer his people, and he will do so "in righteousness." As David prayed for God to continue to act on Israel's behalf, he was certain that God would answer according to his will. David also expresses this confidence in the second half of verse 5, confessing that God is "the hope of all the ends of the earth and of the farthest seas." Because of who God is and what he has said, we can always have hope in him.

This is the fundamental lesson which Jesus is teaching through the petition for daily bread: the lesson of trust. Asking God for what we need, we can have the assurance that he will provide because that is what he promised. David says this in Psalm 34:9: "Fear the LORD, you his saints, for those who fear him have no lack!" God our Father has also given his word in Psalm 81:10: "Open your mouth wide, and I will fill it." As we pray in lean times and days of scarcity, we trust that the Father will keep his promise in righteousness.

Banking God's Gifts

The people in Psalm 65 praise God for granting a good harvest. They could look at this material blessing on at least three levels: First, this was God's generosity in the present—proof of his goodness that you could see in the fields and touch with your hands. Second, this was God's faithfulness to his promise in the past—another proof of his word's reliability. And third, this blessing could serve as added assurance for the future. The people could say, "Remember the great harvest that year? Remember how the drought ended with that amazing rainstorm—three days straight—and then the abundance from the fields?"

We should do the same. First, celebrate what God has given today—enjoy his good gifts by sanctifying them with prayer and thanksgiving (1 Tim 4:5). Second, see his blessings as tangible evidence that God faithfully keeps his promises. And third, store it up for the future: make it one more memory of how the Father sustains his children. Remembering his unchanging faithfulness and his rock-solid reliability, we start to understand that we don't have to worry about our money, food, clothing, or health (Matt 6:25–32). We learn that we don't need to doubt that God will provide, for his love endures forever.

We also experience God's gracious provision when he blesses our hard work with success. When we begin to reap the benefits of our labors, it only comes through the Lord (Ps 127:1). Think of all the toil in the background of Psalm 65: the Israelites had been busy ploughing, cultivating, sowing, fertilizing, and irrigating. Like they did every year, they had invested much labor into their crops. But it was all dependent on God's blessings through rain and growth: "You crown the year with your goodness" (v. 11). When we are blessed, we need to keep fighting against a false dependence and misplaced trust. Our confidence is often misdirected; even if we have never said it out loud, the thought can be there, just below the surface: "I'll be OK, because I know how to work hard and I'm resourceful. I'll make it, because I always have my savings." Understanding the nature of our hearts, Jesus teaches us not to trust in ourselves, but only in our Father, the invisible but almighty God who sustains every aspect of our lives with his blessing. It's not our efficiently-running brain that produces our pay every month. It's not the tools in our hand that earn our living, or the skills we have acquired, the business we have built up; it is not our exercising and dieting that keep us healthy. But every gift and opportunity and success are from God—so we thank him for today, and we trust him for tomorrow.

The Bread of Life

God wants us to learn that, as we trust him in temporal things, we can also trust him in things that are eternal. Our daily working, spending, and eating—this is the classroom of faith. God knows that we'll need to visit the supermarket again this week, and that the utility bills should be paid soon. Because he loves you, he will ensure that it can happen. And he supplies these things so that we learn: just as God provides for our bodies, so he will provide for our souls. From the same river that filled all our physical needs— from that same overflowing fountain—we can receive abundant grace and mercy in Christ!

Think of what Jesus said to the woman sitting at the well in John 4. He told her, "Everyone who drinks of this water will be thirsty again" (v. 13). The stuff of this life will only last so long. We will eat dinner this evening, but we'll need to eat again tomorrow morning. We might have some fine earthly goods right now, but they will fade. Our car will rust. Our home will crumble. Our phone will soon be obsolete (if it isn't already). Even our bodies and minds are going to wear out. Nothing earthly can permanently satisfy our longings or provide an unfailing security, yet in God's grace we have an everlasting hope. This is what Jesus declared: "Whoever drinks of the water that I will give him will never be thirsty again. The water that I will give him will become in him a spring of water welling up to eternal life" (v. 14). True and lasting life comes only from him.

This is a truth to ponder as we enjoy another meal or earn another paycheck. We might have our daily bread today, even immeasurably more than we need, but if we're not eating from Jesus, the Bread of Life, then it's a waste. We might have all our physical desires supplied—even live in a kind of luxury—but if we have not been made rich in Christ, it's all for nothing. God has given this physical life so that we will seek him, turn to Christ in faith, and serve him as our Lord. So let us learn to praise God for what we most value: praise him for our daily bread, and praise him for the Bread of Life!

Reflection and Discussion Questions

1. Reflect on what you most often praise God for in your prayers. Does this indicate anything about what you value most? Perhaps even what you value too much?

2. Why does Christ teach us to ask for "our *daily* bread" and not "our *weekly* bread?"

3. Take some time to recount what God has given you recently. In general, what is your response to the good gifts of God the Father?

4. How should God's giving shape your giving? What are ways in which you can be more generous to others?

5. What does it mean to be content (e.g., Phil 4:11–13; 1 Tim 6:7–8)? How have you been learning to be content with God's gifts?

6. How are you satisfied by Jesus, the Bread of Life? (John 6:35)

CHAPTER 7

Forgiven and Changed

Unchanging Grace

THERE ARE MANY THINGS that can be said about the Psalms, but perhaps the most significant is this: they are real. The Psalms are true-to-life, personal expressions of what moves in the hearts of God's children as we live in covenant with him through Christ. Reading this ancient book of prayers, we can relate to their different moods. There are occasions when we gladly echo the thanksgiving of Psalm 100, share the exuberant joy of Psalm 150, or pray with the quiet trust of Psalm 46. Taking them into our hearts and onto our lips, these are profound prayers that we ourselves can offer.

But we echo sadder psalms, too. For the Psalms don't always give voice to the happy spirit of a person who is walking close to God; they also express the anguish of sin and the burden of guilt. Among these prayers, we hear the pain, regret, and shame of a wickedness that has long been concealed. There is even the fear that a grievous sin has broken a person's fellowship with God, and it cannot be fixed. For instance, we hear the anguished words of Psalm 51: "For I know my transgressions, and my sin is ever before me. Against you, you only, have I sinned and done what is evil in your sight" (vv. 3–4). These repentant words are painfully true to our own experience, and they are echoed whenever we humbly pray as Jesus taught in the fifth petition of the Lord's Prayer:

"Forgive us our debts" (Matt 6:12). Regrettably, it is a prayer we must offer up time and again: "O Lord, forgive me. Please do not cast me away because of my sin, but have mercy."

Whenever we are sunk under the weight of a sinner's guilt and misery, we need to keep reading, because there is always hope—there is a lot of sin, but there is even more grace. The same David who poured out his broken heart in Psalm 51:3–4 is speaking to God with courage a few verses later: "Restore to me the joy of your salvation, and uphold me with a willing spirit" (v. 12). We join him in this plea, and yet our prayers are even richer and our comfort deeper because we know Jesus Christ! In him, we give our "Amen" to David's words of confession—not just in Psalm 51, but also Psalm 32, as we will see—identifying with his hurt and his hope, and giving thanks for a mercy made surer in Jesus's blood.

Our Psalm

For some of the Psalms, we know the circumstances that gave rise to their words. Psalm 51, for example, bears the detailed heading: "A Psalm of David, when Nathan the prophet went to him, after he had gone in to Bathsheba." This is something we can easily picture. We see King David stricken with sorrow and guilt—perhaps collapsed on the floor of his palace—still in those dark days after committing adultery and then ordering Uriah to be killed in a desperate cover-up attempt (2 Sam 11). We hear David's anguished cries echoing throughout the palace halls, "Have mercy on me, O God, according to your steadfast love; according to your abundant mercy blot out my transgressions" (51:1).

When it comes to Psalm 32, however, we are given no window into the events behind it. The heading simply says that this is a psalm of David, "A Maskil." The precise meaning of this term is unclear, but in the NKJV it is translated "A Contemplation." To contemplate something is to consider it carefully, to turn it over in your mind. This word certainly suits the content of Psalm 32; instead of being wracked with guilt over one particular offense, David seems to be reflecting broadly on his many sins. And it may even be preferable that we don't know the situation behind Psalm 32, for sometimes we read the anguish of Psalm 51 with a sense of detachment. We think about King David abusing his God-given position of authority in order to commit adultery with his neighbor's wife, orchestrating the murder of her husband, being reckless in doing whatever he pleased—and perhaps we think to ourselves, "I'm definitely a sinner, but I would never do that! Even if I wanted to, I couldn't sin like he did, because of his position as king." It's not legitimate, but we try to put a safe distance between Psalm 51 and ourselves.

But there is no avoiding Psalm 32. This psalm deflates our pride, and it doesn't allow us to quibble about greater and lesser sins. There is no one who can read it and say, "I can't relate, for I wouldn't do that." We are *all* sinners, and sinners in such an ugly diversity of ways! This hard truth is demonstrated, for instance, by how David uses four different words for sin in just the first two verses: transgression, sin, iniquity, and deceit. In this contemplation, he is taking a full inventory of his heart. He peers into every dark corner, and in every corner he sees sin. If we're honest with ourselves and honest before God, Psalm 32 is "our" psalm, too. These ancient words supply the headline for our lives: we are guilty.

The Pain of Guilt

One way in which we know that guilt is real is because the pain is real. David describes how he was becoming physically sick because of his guilt: "When I kept silent, my bones wasted away through my groaning all day long" (Ps 32:3). He felt like his bones were rotting, like his body was coming apart at the seams—not because of cancer, broken bones, or old age, but because of sin. His sin was eating him up. This can sound strange to us, for what does an intangible, "spiritual" thing like guilt have to do with our physical bodies? Countless scans at the hospital are never going to reveal any sin-spots or guilt-tumors. We might say that David is just imagining things about how sin was affecting his body and making it waste away. He was a holy hypochondriac!

Yet remember how God created us: a unity of body and soul. We are not two separate and distinct parts, but we are one complete person made in God's image (Gen 1:26-27). This means that there is always an intimate connection between the inward and outward parts, between spirit and flesh. If we are afflicted on the inside, even if we're just thinking about something acutely negative, our whole life can feel rotten, as if our very body and bones are weakened. Guilt can gnaw away at our heart, sin can unsettle our life— and particularly unconfessed sin. This is what David is describing: "When I kept silent, my bones grew old" (Ps 32:3, NKJV). When there is a sin we have not acknowledged—when we're dragging it around because we haven't brought it to the Lord—then we're going to feel it. It becomes hard to pray. There is no joy in daily blessings. Worship feels empty. In everything there are shadows. If we do not confess our sin, the burden is only going to get heavier and the lingering ache will only get worse.

And this is not a punishment, it is God's mercy! David knows who is afflicting him, for he prays, "Day and night *your hand* was heavy upon me" (v. 4). Feeling the sting of guilt, feeling a hot iron burning into our conscience is—in a certain sense—a very good thing. It is God's hand, heavy but gracious. It is his hand, correcting us, disciplining us, urging us to return. When we cannot feel that hand anymore, we should worry. When we have become numb to sin after so many failures, when we're not shocked by its ugliness, we should be deeply concerned. It can be fatal if we've come to a place where we are OK with living apart from God, when blatant sinning no longer bothers us. But if sin still hurts and grieves our soul, then we know God is mercifully pulling us back.

According to David, this is what God's gracious chastising feels like: "My strength was dried up as by the heat of summer" (v. 4). Guilt for sin paralyzed David, left him with no desire to keep going and no appetite for life. It is deeply miserable, but this is God the Father patiently teaching, lovingly disciplining (Prov 3:11-12; Heb 12:3-11). God wants us to understand the fundamentals of life, that if we're not right with him, there really is nothing right. What is the point of our life, if we are not walking with the true

God and trusting the Savior? There is no point. Without God's intervention, we are wretched, hopeless captives to a cruel master (Rom 6:12). Without God's grace through Jesus, the guilt that eats away at us now will consume us forever.

Full Disclosure

The difficulty of sincerely praying this petition is that we often try to hide our sins. We might be miserable and guilty, but we don't want to admit it. We try to cover up our transgressions, even under fine layers of outward religion: being nice, singing along at church, saying all the right things when people ask. But this is like wallpapering the moldy walls in a damp bathroom—it's not a solution. The mold is still there, and it will grow and destroy.

Instead of deceiving ourselves, we must look straight into the mirror of God's word in Psalm 32 and see ourselves rightly. Even as church-going and Bible-reading Christians, this is who we are truly: people fatally marred by transgression, sin, iniquity, and deceit. In us there is a close-clinging evil which endures like the most stubborn stain (Heb 12:1). We can't get rid of it by our own efforts in holiness and religiosity—only God can address the problem of our sin. It is clear that David understands this in Psalm 32, crying out to the Lord in the midst of his pain: "I acknowledged my sin to you, and I did not cover my iniquity" (v. 5). Acknowledging sin to God means no more smokescreen, no more hiding, but full disclosure.

In orderly to properly pray "forgive us our debts," we need to be specific. Jesus calls us to contemplate our sin, to reflect on our shortcomings, and take an inventory of our transgressions. And we shouldn't only think about the "big sins," the major blunders we made, the terrible wrongs we committed and which still might cause a pang of guilty shame. There are probably several (thousand) of those. But we should also think broadly about our life and everything that fills it. Where is the sin in the routine of my everyday activity? What are my failings in how I treat my wife, my husband, my children, my friends? How am I showing pride? How am I ungrateful to God, or how do I neglect him at the expense of my idols? What love haven't I shown to my neighbors? We ought to mull over these things, not because we sadistically want to feel the pain of guilt, or because we believe that low self-esteem is good for us. We confess sin in order to take the first steps toward a renewal of joy, for when we truly acknowledge our transgressions, the Father promises that we'll experience the delight of his gracious pardon (1 John 1:9).

The Joy of Release

Psalm 32 is marked by a marvelous transformation. This is a distressed prayer filled with anguished words; the pain is raw, yet notice the opening notes of David's song: "Blessed is the one whose transgression is forgiven, whose sin is covered" (v. 1). Before he says anything else about his misery, David begins with blessedness. He cannot suppress this happy impulse because, as a child of God, he has already tasted the goodness of God's grace, and he knows that he's being renewed by the Spirit of the Lord. As a result, this new life comes bursting out of him, expressed in song and prayer!

Imagine a prisoner, confined to jail: a serial killer, a dangerous offender, the worst of the worst. He has been tried, condemned, and sentenced to life in prison, with little chance of parole. Society has given up on transforming him or rehabilitating him into someone safe and productive. But where we give up, God does not. For God can take a hardened criminal and transform him; by God's decla-ration, his very status is changed from "guilty" to "righteous." God even sets the prisoner free from his deserved captivity, and he tells him, "Go and sin no more" (John 5:14). In God's courtroom, the convicted criminal is us. We are the dangerous offender, the worst of sinners—and God's justice gives him every reason to lock us up with everlasting chains. But God the righteous Judge does not continue to charge us with sin. This is the miracle of God's grace: my sin and sinfulness don't go on my record, and they are not held against me! Instead, by faith in Christ, I have been transformed from guilty to righteous (Rom 8:1).

It is good to read David's words in Psalm 32:5 again: "I acknowledged my sin to you, and I did not cover my iniquity; I said, 'I will confess my transgressions to the LORD,'" and—wait for the miracle—"*and you forgave the iniquity of my sin*." Whatever grievous wrongs David committed, whatever ugly things he uncovered in his inventory of sin, God has cleared them away. Even the countless things that David was not aware of, the innumerable sins that escaped his notice—even these God has graciously pardoned: "You forgave the iniquity of my sin."

What does this forgiveness really mean? Forgiveness means the Father doesn't let our sins from yesterday affect the way he treats us today. Forgiveness means that God won't keep reminding us about how we failed—it's as if he has forgotten our sins entirely (Isa 43:25). God casts our wickedness into the deepest part of the sea (Mic 7:18–19); he puts all our sins behind his back (Isa 38:17); he removes our transgressions from us, as far as the east is from the west (Ps 103:12). God regards us with his profoundly transforming love, with the result that our relationship with him is unstained by any evil we have done, whether it was done twenty years ago or earlier today.

This is the joy of release that David experienced and which prompted his opening words of praise. God's forgiveness means the lifting of an unbearable weight, the melting of a painful tension. If we are burdened by guilt and all the wrong things we have done, what an amazing gift it is to talk with God again and to walk with him—to have no more fear of his condemnation, but instead a sure hope for renewed fellowship with the Father! It is the unspeakable joy of God's grace, and it is not far away for those who humbly ask.

For Jesus's Sake

We don't like to say that we are superior to David, or that we have it better than the saints of the Old Testament. But we do, for how much stronger can be our confidence in the grace of God our Father through Christ! It is like we get to read Psalm 32 while wearing a set of precision-crafted glasses. They are glasses focused by the New Testament, glasses that constantly set before us the person and work of Jesus. We see what he did to accomplish our salvation, how he became the guilty one so that we could be declared innocent. Far better than David could understand, we know how God at his own expense made costly arrangements to pay the full penalty for all our sin. Without Jesus, sinners don't have a hope or a prayer, but for the sake of his blood we have peace with God (Rom 5:1).

This is why we often add the phrase "for Jesus's sake" to our prayers. As is true for every component of prayer, this closing expression can easily become an afterthought or an empty habit. To remind ourselves of the sole basis for prayer, we should reflect on the world of meaning that is wrapped up in this little phrase: "For Jesus's sake, please hear this prayer. Father, do not answer me because of me. Answer and forgive, for the sake of Christ's blood." Christ is the only reason that we can call God our Father (John 1:12). Jesus is the only way into God's holy presence (John 14:6). When we pray for forgiveness with confidence through Christ, God will bless us with a renewal of joy.

It is on the high note of "rejoicing in the Lord" that Psalm 32 ends. After the distress of guilt and the pain of being far from God's gracious presence, David invites all of God's children: "Be glad in the LORD, and rejoice, O righteous, and shout for joy, all you upright in heart!" (v. 11). We can be glad, because healing is available for our rotten bones and our broken spirit. No longer must we live in the misery of our sin, but we can rejoice that God's forgiveness relieves our burdened hearts and grants true peace (Matt 11:28–30).

New Resolve

We are learning to cherish God's gift of forgiveness, but we're not there yet. I once heard a good comparison for how Christians treat this gift. The person recounted that he once had a dog as a pet and faithful companion; at the time, he lived in the English countryside, with many puddles and ditches nearby. Like any good owner, he would give his dog a regular bath. But no sooner was his dog washed and dried and carefully brushed than it would go and frolic in a pool of dirty water or muck. It was a frustratingly short-lived cleanliness! After a while, the long-suffering owner gave up on his dog's monthly bath. Lamentably, we often live like that dog. We get grace from God, receive cleansing from sin, and then simply return to the wrongs we were previously doing. We commit the same sin we committed yesterday; we continue to neglect Scripture or disregard prayer, or we don't really do anything to combat our anger or lust or envy. The sin is still there, still alive. At the day's end, we will ask for forgiveness, but tomorrow we will frolic again in the filth that surrounds us and blithely accept the corruption that still clings to us.

This is not how it should be, for having been cleansed, there should be a transformation. David exhorts us in his psalm: "Be not like a horse or a mule, without understanding, which must be curbed with bit and bridle, or it will not stay near you" (32:9). He understands that we're inclined to be stubborn and keep traveling the same wrong path that we were on before. Like farmyard animals, it's as if we need to be compelled and forced to do God's will, otherwise we'll bolt. But grace changes us. After our cleansing with Christ's blood and Spirit, it is God's will that we move forward in a better direction and walk freely in the paths of righteousness and holiness. Because of this need for transformation, David is doing two central things in Psalm 32. First, he is asking for forgiveness, as we've seen already. And second, he is asking for instruction, for lessons in how to live as someone who is holy and forgiven and completely dedicated to God.

God answers this request for holy counsel, for David records the Lord's word to him: "I will instruct you and teach you in the way you should go; I will counsel you with my eye upon you" (v. 8). This remains the only way that we will learn God's truth, if he will teach us and instruct us in his will. So this must be our prayer:

"Father, forgive my sins. And Father, please teach me how *not* to sin. Teach me to avoid this temptation and beat this weakness, to put off the works of my old nature and put on what is new and holy (Col 3:5–17). Enable me to do what is right and good." This is comparable to what David prays in Psalm 51: "Create in me a clean heart, O God, and renew a right spirit within me" (v. 10). After confessing and being forgiven, the child of God asks for a new resolve to pursue holiness and a changed disposition toward the Lord and his will.

It is a fundamental Scriptural truth that renewal of life always accompanies God's forgiving grace (Rom 12:1–2; Eph 4:1). If we have been shown forgiving mercy, God's grace will be seen in how we desire worship and maintain prayer. His grace will be seen in how we strive for a new purity in speech and thought. His grace will be seen in how we try to restore things that we've broken and put right what has been wrong. After we sin and are forgiven, grace is seen in what we do next!

Forgiven and Forgiving Much

The principal life-change that is built right into the Lord's Prayer is our new desire to forgive other people. In the fifth petition, Jesus teaches us to pray: "Forgive us our debts, *as we also have forgiven our debtors*" (Matt 6:12). This means that if someone has offended or hurt us, we should strive to treat them like God has treated us sinners in his generous and patient love. Those who are forgiven much, love much (Luke 7:47). Transgressors who have been treated with divine kindness and compassion ought to "be kind to one another, tender-hearted, forgiving one another, as God in Christ forgave [them]" (Eph 4:32). The mercy which God has poured out on us must overflow in yet more mercy: forgiveness for our husband or wife, for our friends, for other church members, forgiveness even for our enemies.

When God has forgiven us so completely, and so generously—more than we can ever say—why do we still carry around small grudges against other people? After receiving God's amazing grace, we should be prepared to relinquish the resentment that we still hold toward this person or that family. After being forgiven by God so freely and fully, we should not dare to keep bringing up the shortcomings and misdeeds of others, nor should we allow someone's past offenses to affect our relationship today. As imitators of God, we ought to show to all people a God-like patience, compassion, kindness and generosity (Eph 5:1). This kind of spirit and activity are the living evidence of God's grace in us.

The Footprint of Grace

Can the people around us tell that we have been forgiven? Do the people we live with notice that we have received grace? What about the people we work with—do they see that we walk closely with the Lord, depending on his daily mercy? There should be evidence, for God's grace has a footprint, and his compassion leaves a mark. If we have been forgiven, we pray that we'll stop acting like animals. No more should we be like the dog dashing back into the mud puddle; no more should we be like the horse or mule, which have no understanding but depend on bit and bridle. Instead of mindlessly repeating the sins of yesterday and last year, we ought to resolve to change, praying that the Father will show us the path of repentance and forgiveness.

Through praying the fifth petition and receiving God's gracious answer in Christ, the greatest change will be in our relationship with the Lord. David invites us, "Be glad in the LORD, and rejoice, O righteous, and shout for joy, all you upright in heart!" (Ps 32:11). Now that sin's sorrowful and injurious burden has been lifted and we have received the healing of God's Spirit, we rejoice in the Lord and his indescribable mercy (Phil 4:4). We are glad to know him, and we are glad to be known by him. So thank God and rejoice daily for his forgiveness in Jesus Christ!

Reflection and Discussion Questions

1. Why do you think that it is important to be specific in your daily confession of sin? How can you become more specific?

2. Have you ever experienced the pain and destructive power of guilt as David describes in Psalm 32? Tell the story, and how it ended.

3. Scripture presents beautiful images of how God deals with our transgressions. Read Psalm 103:12, Isaiah 44:22, and Micah 7:18–19, and reflect on the miracle of God's forgiving grace.

4. How should receiving God's gift of forgiveness fill you with a new resolve to live in holiness?

5. In relation to the petition "forgive us our debts," what is the lesson of Jesus's parable of the unforgiving servant in Matthew 18:21–35? How do you see this lesson applying to your own relationships?

CHAPTER 8

The War Prayer

Under Christ's Banner

FOR A LONG TIME, the country of my birth has been a fighting nation. Since the late nineteenth century, Canadian troops have gone to war in places like Africa, Europe, and the Middle East. When we consider those who went to fight, it is noticeable that many Christians have enlisted. War can be deadly, but these Christians surely went with the awareness of God's protection, knowing that the Lord was with them in the theaters of war on land, in the air, and on the sea. As these troops went to battle, they went calling on God's name. During World War II, a little booklet called *A Prayer Book for Soldiers and Sailors* was distributed among many English-speaking troops. In it we find this striking petition, entitled "A Morning Prayer":

> Into thy hands, O God, I commend myself this day. Let thy presence be with me even to its close, that at night I may again give thanks unto thee, through Jesus Christ our Lord. Amen. Grant, O Lord, that I may not be ashamed to confess the faith of Christ crucified, and manfully to fight under his banner against sin, the world, and the devil, and to continue Christ's faithful soldier and servant unto my life's end. Amen. Defend, O Lord, this thy Child with thy heavenly grace; that I may continue thine

forever; and daily increase in thy Holy Spirit more and
more, until I come unto thy everlasting kingdom. Amen.

These words are a powerful confession of reliance on the Lord. It's
easy to imagine a Christian soldier earnestly offering up such a
prayer just before another mission or perilous day at the frontline.

Today, not many of us wear the uniform of our nation or fight
overseas against foreign armies. But we are still soldiers, fighting
under the banner of Christ. In the spiritual war that is this present
life, we have unswerving enemies who are attacking us. This means
that we too, need "a prayer book for soldiers," and we too, need
to ask for God's daily help and care. This is precisely what Jesus
teaches in the last petition of the Lord's Prayer, "Lead us not into
temptation, but deliver us from evil" (Matt 6:13), a war prayer that
echoes the words of Psalm 35.

A Hate-filled Enemy

Soldiers sometimes wonder at the intense hatred shown by their
enemies, for it goes beyond the level of having a reasonable stra-
tegic purpose and nearly resembles fanaticism. People can be so
blinded by their ideology that they stop at nothing to further their
cause and destroy the enemy.

This is the kind of brutal opposition that David was facing
in Psalm 35. While it is another psalm for which we don't know
the exact circumstances, clearly David's life was in danger from an
enemy who is full of hatred and deceit. It's possible that this psalm
is from the years when David was being hounded by King Saul,
but even once he took the throne David had many enemies, both
foreign nations and people from his own household. Indeed, in
Psalm 35, it sounds like David was being oppressed by men who
were once close to him but are now desperate to kill him.

In the opening verse of his war prayer, David cries out: "Contend, O LORD, with those who contend with me; fight against
those who fight against me!" (v. 1). His enemies are seeking his
life, trying to trap him, and persecuting him fiercely. They are

tenacious in their attacks on him as the Lord's servant, for as soon as David takes a misstep, they are ready to assault him: "But at my stumbling they rejoiced and gathered; they gathered together against me; wretches whom I did not know tore at me without ceasing" (v. 15). David faces a determined and dangerous enemy who will not rest until he is dead.

Already we see how David's prayer is instructive to us. For the reality is that we are always under attack by an adversary who hates us. There might not be angry people banging against the church doors, we probably don't face accusations in court because of our Christian faith, and likely our property isn't being taken away. Yet there is an enemy moving against us; we cannot physically see him, but he is there. Paul describes our present situation: "For we do not wrestle against flesh and blood, but against the rulers, against the authorities, against the cosmic powers over this present darkness, against the spiritual forces of evil in the heavenly places" (Eph 6:12). As disciples of Christ, we have adversaries—and they are not some friendly competition, like the opposing team on the playing field. These are not foes who attack, engage in battle for a while, and then lose interest, but they are fanatical enemies, filled with a hatred of a marked intensity. They have a total dedication to our destruction, wanting to ruin our faith and capture our souls.

The Axis of Evil

For centuries, Christians have identified an axis of evil that is stirring against the church, an unholy trinity: the devil, the world, and our own sinful flesh. The devil, of course, is the mastermind, the general in charge of all the battalions of darkness. Daily he plots and schemes and invents new ways of doing the same old sins. He can make sin seem most pleasant, easy, and private. He can make it feel like the most natural and justifiable thing. By whatever temptation he can devise, Satan will sidetrack us. And he doesn't let himself be pushed away easily, but returns constantly with new strategies. His temptations are all designed to draw us away from the Lord and to ruin the church, which is why, in his letter, James counsels: "Resist the devil, and he will flee from you" (4:7). It is imperative that we do not make peace with Satan, but fight hard against his deceptive attacks with the truth of God's word.

The world—the world where we live and move and work—is happy to cooperate with the devil. The unbelieving world in rebellion against God serves as the willing vehicle for Satan to deliver his explosives: planting temptation along the roads we travel daily, carrying falsehood to the doorstep of the church, even bringing his evil right into our homes. As the apostle John warns, "All that is in the world—the desires of the flesh and the desires of the eyes and pride of life—is not from the Father but is from the world" (1 John 2:16). With a godless world as our enemy, the battle lines are not in a foreign land across the ocean, but are uncomfortably close. This reality is reflected in Jesus's prayer to the Father for his believers in John 17:15: "I do not ask that you take them out of the world, but that you keep them from the evil one." While we are living in this world, the combat will be real.

We even have an enemy in our own sinful flesh. David had his betrayers, but this killer is the ultimate traitor. God has recreated us and given us new birth by his Holy Spirit, but the lingering remnants of our sinful nature still side with the enemy (cf. Rom 7:15–20). "Just try it," our hearts whisper. "No one will know about this sin. No one else is saying no to this. You deserve this pleasure." Like the most deranged suicide bomber, our sinful flesh seems hell-bent on self-destruction. Consequently, every day we have to fight against the stubborn pull of our hearts, like the Holy Spirit exhorts in Colossians 3:5, "Put to death therefore what is earthly in you." Kill your sin, before it kills you!

Temptations on the Radar

Having identified our enemies, we need to calibrate our spiritual radars to detect all their temptations, both great and small. This vigilance is necessary, because it is particularly easy to classify as "temptations" the heinous sins that everyone will agree are wrong, like the temptation to have an affair with the woman in our small group at church or to steal money from our employer. Such temptations can be terrifyingly intense and must be resisted fiercely. But we should also recognize that our enemy's temptations can be far more subtle, and far less outwardly offensive. Temptation is as simple as the urge to share unpleasant news about someone who hurt us in the past. It's as "harmless" as the habit of spitting out harsh or critical words without a moment's deliberation. Temptation is as natural as our willingness to let easier things take the place of Scripture-reading. Temptation is as covert as a stolen glance at someone else's body, as quick as a fury-filled outburst at our child, and as subtle as a proud or envious thought. We hardly notice it. The point is, temptation flies under the radar, stealthily penetrating when our attention is elsewhere.

How often are we tempted? It is not just here and there, it's constant. We must not let down our guard when living in this ungodly world, nor expect the devil to give us a free pass, nor trust our hearts to make the right decision. We are always on the field of battle! And as we said, the complicating factor in this battle is that we are so weak, so fearful, so prone to attack. David knew his weakness—this is why he poured out his heart to God in Psalm 35. He was bowed down and nearly broken, so he humbled himself in verse 17: "How long, O Lord, will you look on? Rescue me from their destruction, my precious life from the lions!"

We should join David, praying in our inherent vulnerability. We should admit that we are likely to surrender at the slightest attack, that we drop our guard the moment things start looking comfortable, that we yield to the gentlest suggestion. We can't stand even for a moment! In ourselves we are helpless, but with our Ally we have an unfailing strength. Like David sang about another battle he once faced, "If it had not been the LORD who was on our side—let Israel now say—if it had not been the LORD who was on our side when people rose up against us, then they would have swallowed us up alive" (Ps 124:1–3). This is how critical our situation is, and how essential is God's help.

An Almighty Ally

If a nation is looking to launch an invasion or fend off an attack, she will typically look for allies. Because fighting a war demands many resources, you need others to join and support you. In our spiritual war, God is an ally who is both almighty and reliable. Remember how David begins his war prayer in Psalm 35: "Contend, O LORD, with those who contend with me; fight against those who fight against me!" (v. 1). This is a request that God will fight his battles, that he will take up David's cause against his enemies—even that God will destroy those foes completely!

Most of us are peace-loving people, so we might be uncertain if this is really a proper thing to pray, asking God to fight for us. We must pray according to God's will, for the things that he has commanded in his word—so is this one of his promises, that God will be a warrior on our behalf? But David knows how God has revealed himself, such as when the Lord showed his soldierly identity at the Red Sea and destroyed the mighty army of the Egyptians. Moses sang back then, "The LORD is a man of war; the LORD is his name. Pharaoh's chariots and his host he cast into the sea, and his chosen officers were sunk in the Red Sea" (Exod 15:3–4). The Lord is a man of war—a warrior, constantly defending and fighting for his people! Against the Amalekites, against the Syrians, against the Moabites, against the Philistines, against the Midianites, against countless enemies, God has waged war and won. So David is right to pray—*we* are right to pray—"Fight against those who fight against me."

Our God's soldierly spirit is also reflected in the sixth petition: "Lead us not into temptation, but deliver us from evil." Jesus teaches us to pray that God will accompany us into the theaters of war, that he will save and protect us, his weak and wobbly troops. By God's power we can overcome the devil; with his strength, God "will soon crush Satan under [our] feet" (Rom 16:20). For Satan might have a well-defined purpose, but he is not invincible; he might be intelligent, but he is not perfectly wise; he may have freedom to tempt, but he is still under Christ's control. We must not underestimate the devil—that could be fatal—but we do know God's power: "There is none like you, O LORD; you are great, and your name is great in might" (Jer 10:6). So we should pray that he will keep Satan's power in check, restrain this sinful world, and keep transforming our traitorous hearts.

God is a Warrior

At the beginning of a new day, before Satan's bullets and bombs start flying, before navigating the minefields of personal relationships and ethical conflicts, we should pray that our warrior God will uphold and strengthen us. This is how David pleads with God: "Take hold of shield and buckler and rise for my help! Draw the spear and javelin against my pursuers!" (Ps 35:2–3). Notice that David actually portrays God as a fighter, a soldier decked out with armor. The Lord has a shield and a buckler—a small round shield worn on the arm for warding off attacks—and he is wielding a spear and javelin for going on the offensive. He is ready to fight!

Military imagery for God also occurs elsewhere in the Bible. There is the description of the Lord in Isaiah 59:17: "He put on righteousness as a breastplate, and a helmet of salvation on his head; he put on garments of vengeance for clothing and wrapped himself in zeal as a cloak." Or think of Habakkuk 3:8–15, which speaks of God's chariot of war, his bow and arrows, and his glittering spear—all being brought against his foes in order to crush and pierce. Scripture shows God as equipped and prepared for a fight—you wouldn't want to meet him in a dark alley or on a battlefield. To quote the well-known line from C. S. Lewis's *The Lion, the Witch, and the Wardrobe*, where Mr. Beaver describes the great lion Aslan: "'Safe?' said Mr. Beaver . . . 'Who said anything about safe? 'Course he isn't safe. But he's good. He's the king, I tell you.'" God is a great warrior—not safe, but good—who is able and ready to fight for his chosen ones. Ask him to help, and he will! In our deep-seated struggles against the power of sin, against our own weakness and the pressures of this world, we can pray with David: "Fight against those who fight against me." And God will fight.

This is the God who will give the courage to stand up against evil, even when it feels like we are standing all alone. He will grant the wisdom to see through Satan's deception, even when his lies are so convincing. God will supply strength in the moment of temptation, even when everything inside us wants to succumb. He will show the way of escape from sin and teach the path of righteousness instead. If we ask him to, he will fight for us on every front, taking hold of shield and buckler, drawing out the spear, and stopping those who pursue us.

Armored Up

Seeing God as a great warrior reminds us of the spiritual armor described in Ephesians 6. After Paul alerts us to the high stakes of our battle against the powers of darkness, he urges us to be ready for battle, but not with physical things like body armor or assault rifles. Instead, he says, "Take up the whole armor of God, that you may be able to withstand in the evil day, and having done all, to stand firm" (v. 13). Notice that he speaks about the armor *of God*; this is not just the armor that God gives his people, but the armor that the almighty God himself wears—his breastplate, his helmet, his garments. This armor will surely be effective!

If we are going to stand firm in this fight, then we must be ready. Part of every soldier's basic training is weapons instruction; a soldier must know how to handle firearms and explosives in order to be an effective fighter. Similarly, the good soldier for Christ walks in step with his commander and never leaves home without his armor. If we are facing temptations every day, if we are constantly dealing with the lies of the devil and the attacks of this world, and if we are always trying to ignore the subtle whispers of our own heart, we need armor.

We must be fastening tight the belt of truth by knowing God's sanctifying truth. We must be strapping on the breastplate of righteousness by living in the righteousness of Christ. We must be tying up the sandals of the gospel by loving the gospel, and taking in hand the shield of faith by growing our faith. Let us put on the helmet of salvation by seeing our new identity in Christ our Savior. And we must take up the sword of the Spirit—we will only be able to stand fast if we know the Scriptures, the sole truth that can defeat the devil's lie. If we are faithfully putting on this armor, we can make this our prayer: "Fight against those who fight against me!" In ourselves we are weak and vulnerable, just an unguarded instant away from falling, yet through Christ we can "be strong in the Lord and in the strength of his might" (Eph 6:10) and sure of our victory through him.

Confident of Victory

When a country's troops are fighting overseas, one of the topics for constant debate in the halls of government and in the press is the war's potential outcome. Will we achieve a clear victory? That is often the question, especially when there is news of another battle badly lost. In his warfare, however, David had great confidence of success. This comes out in his prayer in Psalm 35:3 when he asks of God, "Say to my soul, 'I am your salvation!'" David yearned to hear the good news of victory, and he knew that God would not disappoint.

In a similar way, the Christian soldier today—you and me and every believer—can pray in sure confidence. There is no question about the outcome, for in Christ we have already won! This is not over-confidence: it is recognizing the perfect power of the mighty God who fights for us. Think of how God encouraged Joshua, the great warrior for God's people more than three millennia ago. Joshua was facing a long and arduous conquest of the promised land; Canaan was populated by great and numerous enemies, while Israel was just a nation of shepherds and farmers. But this is what God said: "Be strong and courageous. Do not be frightened, and do not be dismayed, for the LORD your God is with you wherever you go" (Josh 1:9). Joshua received confirmation that God was his almighty ally, just as he later received words of assurance from the angelic commander of the army of the Lord (Josh 6:14). Up against what seemed like impossible odds, Joshua knew that the outcome of this campaign was not in doubt and that God would fight his battles.

We know the same heartening truth—so what will we do when we need to stick up for what is right, when we are tempted to conform to the pattern of the world, or when we face the choice between doing God's will and our own? We can march with courage, wearing the full armor of God and fighting with the certainty of victory. When it comes to Christ's church, the devil must admit defeat. He knows who is on our side; he knows he can only go so far, and no more. This can give us confidence in our daily battles, for when we humbly resist the devil with God's power, the victory is ours!

Maybe you have seen pictures of what took place at the end of World War II when victory in Europe was declared. Hundreds of thousands of people filled the streets and celebrated, for the unimaginable had happened, and the war was finally over. Rejoicing shines through in Psalm 35 as well, for David knows that God will put a song of praise on his lips, "Great is the LORD, who delights in the welfare of his servant! Then my tongue shall tell of your righteousness and of your praise all the day long" (vv. 27–28). In Christ, we have the joy of victory, the gladness of knowing the Lord and his total triumph.

Keep Praying

Today and tomorrow and for the rest of our earthly life, we will face the heat of battle. Wherever we go, whatever we do, we need help: strength, courage, and wisdom. So we need to keep praying. If we are going to take part in that final victory celebration, we must pray diligently, fervently, and constantly! Notice how it is prayer that receives the most attention in Paul's words in Ephesians 6 about our fight against the evil one. After listing the different pieces of armor, prayer is how he concludes his exhortation—for prayer is like the structure underneath which will keep it all together. In the thick of our spiritual warfare, he exhorts us: "Pray in the Spirit on all occasions with all kinds of prayers and requests. With this in mind, be alert and always keep on praying for all the Lord's people" (v. 18, NIV). This is a reminder that ultimate success rests not on our efforts and vigilance, but on the strength of the Lord God alone. So let us pray for ourselves, and pray also "for all the Lord's people," for our brothers and sisters in Christ, for those going through the same kind of temptations. Pray for the Spirit's transformation to continue and for our daily battles to be won more and more often.

"Watch and pray," says Jesus (Matt 26:41), and "pray and work." Work at resisting the deadly deceits of the devil. Work at overcoming the world's pressure to conform. Work at putting to death the stubborn desires of your sinful heart. Do all this under Christ's banner and in Christ's power until his final victory!

Reflection and Discussion Questions

1. In what ways does your life resemble "a spiritual war?" (See Eph 6:12.)

2. Is it God who tempts us? (See Jas 1:13.) What then, are we asking for when we pray to him, "Lead us not into temptation"?

3. In Psalm 144:1, David speaks about how God trains his hands for war. How can you be trained? And how can you be equipped with the armor of God (Eph 6:13–17)?

4. Does God always keep the promise of 1 Corinthians 10:13? Has he kept it, even when you have fallen into sin? Reflect on a recent experience of fighting temptation.

5. Think about what you can learn about resisting the devil's temptations from the example of Jesus in Matthew 4:1–11.

6. In the daily clash with sin, how are you encouraged by the promise of Christ's final victory over our enemies?

CHAPTER 9

A Finale of Praise and Confidence

Not with a Bang but a Whimper

ANY MUSICIAN WILL AGREE that the opening notes of a song are crucial—you want to nail the first few bars, because everything that follows builds on a good opening. In the same way, the opening of a prayer expresses much about our conversation with the Lord. Jesus teaches us to begin our prayers well, starting our communion with God in the right spirit. The good beginning is in those simple words of address, "Our Father who is in heaven," a phrase that express humble reverence and loving trust. Closely following this appropriate start come the three God-centered petitions: "Hallowed be your name," "Your kingdom come," and "Your will be done."

Maybe we begin well, but by the end of our prayer we are sometimes losing our focus. By the end we might be getting impatient with sitting still, growing eager to tackle whatever is next in our day. Maybe we're even falling asleep as we conclude our prayer. If my own prayers are any indication, I fear that the end is often something like a feeble dwindling. There might be a perfunctory addition of a few familiar phrases and some generalized requests in order to wrap it up while we push onwards to the final "Amen."

Is it really important, the conclusion of our speaking with the Father? Should we offer sincere and meaningful words to God from the beginning to the very end of our prayer? The answer should be obvious: of course the ending of our prayers is important! We know that every word enters God's heavenly throne room, and that for Jesus's sake the Father hears each one of his children. The ending can express much meaning, even as much as the beginning, so a finale of praise and confidence is fitting. In this good spirit, with these last notes lingering in our hearts, we carry on with other things for a time. This is the lesson of the conclusion of the Lord's Prayer: "For yours is the kingdom and the power and the glory, forever. Amen" (Matt 6:13). In these final components of a God-pleasing prayer, we will see how Christ's model prayer again echoes the praise and confidence of the Psalms, such as Psalm 41 and 147.

Bookends of Praise

Many Christians grow up learning that the chief purpose of our lives here on earth is to glorify God. Like the Reformation taught us, and as Bach reminded us, *Soli Deo Gloria*. It is imperative that we honor the triune God by the way we think, the words we speak, and how we behave each and every day. This life purpose implies that our daily prayers must also glorify the Lord. You could say that we're called to pray in the same way that we live, in humble adoration of our God in heaven.

Jesus taught us to begin our prayers with the pace-setting petition "Hallowed be your name." Our daily prayer is that the Father would be glorified in and through us, his little children. We want him to be glorified in our life—in our families, in our church, in our weekly work and responsibilities, in our times of leisure and rest. We start our prayer with a petition for God to be exalted, and we're taught to end our prayers in the same way, with a beautiful doxology: "For yours is the kingdom and the power and the glory, forever." Notice how the two bookends of Jesus's perfect prayer are praise and worship.

A Doxological People

Christ instructed us to finish our prayers with a doxology, which is a brief formula or statement of praise. The most well-known doxology might be the hymn found in myriad songbooks throughout Christendom:

> Praise God, from whom all blessings flow;
> Praise him, all creatures here below;
> Praise him above, ye heavenly host;
> Praise Father, Son, and Holy Ghost. Amen.

But doxologies aren't found only in the hymnbooks of the New Testament church. For many centuries, God's covenant people have been offering up these short yet powerful declarations of his greatness in order to hallow his name.

For instance, consider the doxology placed at the end of Psalm 41: "Blessed be the LORD, the God of Israel, from everlasting to everlasting!" (v. 13). There is also a doxology bracketing Psalm 147, a simple cry of worship that is heard both at the beginning and at the end of this psalm: "Praise the LORD!" Some older English translations of the Bible include what is written literally in the Hebrew, "Hallelujah." This is actually a one-word doxology that is recognizable around the world in countless languages. We know that, at the end of the ages, God's people will still be singing "Hallelujah." Think of the heavenly multitudes that we hear in Revelation: "Hallelujah! For the Lord our God the Almighty reigns!" (19:6). In Psalm 147, this "praise the LORD" exclamation belongs to a majestic doxology of five parts found at the conclusion to the book of Psalms. Each psalm from 146 to 150 is marked by the opening and closing cries of "Praise the Lord." It is remarkable how at the end of the Psalter there is a grand finale of praise, a crescendo of devotion to God.

When you reflect on it, a resounding doxology really is the perfect way to finish the Psalms. As we've been seeing in this book, the Psalms reveal a wide range of circumstances in the lives of God's children, including great joy, deep thankfulness, and quiet trust. But in the Psalms, there is also sorrow, fear, and guilt. By the time a reader arrives at Psalm 150, he has covered much of the undulating terrain of regular life, the constant vicissitudes of a life of faith. Yet throughout this Old Testament prayer book there has been one constant, and that is the Lord: his faithfulness; his power; his love, justice, and steadfast mercy! In every psalm, the expectation and exultation always revert to him. For God's people, the Lord is always our tower of strength (Ps 61:3), our rock of refuge (Ps 71:3), and our sheltering wings (Ps 91:4).

Consequently, there is nothing more appropriate to do at the end of the Psalter than to offer up to God five separate psalms that are shaped by adoration and saturated with worship. As the psalmist teaches in Psalm 147:1, "It is good to sing praises to our God." When we conclude our prayers, it is fitting that we stand back for a moment to let all the attention fall on God. We want to praise, adore, and thank him for we recognize God as who he is, the holy and living God. He is the one who finds great delight in his people's worship.

A Corrective to Self-absorption

This kind of intentional praise is so necessary because we can easily get sidetracked or unfocused when we are in God's presence. While praying, our minds are inclined to wander. For example, we might start dwelling on the sins we have just confessed to God, replaying their pleasures or their shames. Or we might start admiring the gifts we've just thanked the Father for, relishing thoughts of our fine home, our comfortable position, or our promising future. Or as we pray, we might get agitated again by all the troubles burdening our hearts, or we even start looking for new things to worry about! From moment to moment, our thoughts so readily flit back to ourselves, a tendency that can also threaten to derail our prayers.

This is probably one of the greatest dangers for our personal prayers, that they become self-absorbed. The hazard is that a time of prayer becomes a time of ruminating, loosely-connected thinking about the various goings-on of our life. Certainly, we are allowed to pray about these things—it delights the Father when his children present their lives to him in faith. Yet Scripture says that true prayer is communing with God himself, calling on the name of our gracious Father. Engaging in such a privileged activity means we have to keep resetting the mood, keep reorienting our prayers in the proper direction, and keep the spotlight shining on the right person. Life isn't about us and our little kingdom—it's about the Lord God. Praying the doxology is a wonderful way to acknowledge and confess this: "For yours is the kingdom and the power and the glory."

The Chain of Prayer

The first thing to notice in the doxology is the connecting word "for." It is a small but revealing word, which intimates that we're not just tacking on a compliment like the way we might flatter someone in order to get what we want. Praise is not an afterthought, but is part of an unbreakable link in the chain of prayer: "This is what I pray, *for* yours is the kingdom and the power and the glory." Our adoration has everything to do with those things which we've just brought before the Lord. Accordingly, whenever we talk with the Lord, we should acknowledge and confess his majesty and dominion. For instance, with the words of Psalm 147, we can praise the Lord for his greatness: "He determines the number of the stars; he gives to all of them their names. Great is our Lord, and abundant in power; his understanding is beyond measure" (vv. 4–5).

Bringing proper praise requires us to open our closed eyes. As we hurry through life, with our eyes on the ground, on the clock, and on our goals, we stop seeing God's heavenly glory and majesty. We stop recognizing Christ's power at work in the church, such as when his Spirit changes people, and we stop appreciating the Father's grace in the little gifts of each day, such as his protection when we travel. The result is that we take for granted the privilege of approaching God's heavenly throne, and we feel that we are essentially in control, even when we pray. We already have all the necessary strength and ability for this day's labors and challenges—still, we would feel better about things if we prayed, and it might be bad luck if we *didn't* pray. But prayer is much more: it is more than insurance or superstition. For prayer connects us directly to God's perfect strength!

Marvel at everything God does in Psalm 147: "He sends out his command to the earth; his word runs swiftly. He gives snow like wool; he scatters frost like ashes. He hurls down his crystals of ice like crumbs; who can stand before his cold? He sends out his word, and melts them; he makes his wind blow and the waters flow" (vv. 15–18). The psalmist praises the Lord as God of all creation, sovereign over every time and season. God is the director of every event, circumstance, and moment. We cannot do anything without him, and we are lost without his help. Even if we don't acknowledge it like we should, our life is utterly dependent on his blessing, completely contingent on his favor. If we are going to live past this moment, we need God's ever-present power and steadfast mercy!

And God promises to give these very things. For this is his promise in Christ: "The LORD takes pleasure in those who fear him, in those who hope in his steadfast love" (Ps 147:11). Ponder how the Lord God takes thought for us: the one who created everything, governs all, needs nothing and nobody—this God takes true pleasure in those who fear him, and he delights in those who trust him! Our heavenly Father is happy to employ his mighty ability and perfect authority so that he can give us all that is good. As Jesus teaches in his prayer, to God our Father belong "the kingdom and the power and the glory." This is a doxological reminder that God is so much greater than anything here on earth: he is better than all our troubles, he is bigger than all our obstacles, and he is stronger than all our foes and fears. So we can go to God in prayerful expectation and never be disappointed. This promise-keeping God is worthy of prayerful praise and thanksgiving.

Learning to Praise

The Psalms reveal that praise and worship should fill our prayers, that adoration and thanksgiving should be their tone and theme. Whenever we draw near to God, our holy instinct and sanctified habit ought to be offering up a ceaseless and heartfelt doxology. As Psalm 147 says, "It is good to sing praises to our God; for it is pleasant, and a song of praise is fitting" (v. 1). Praise is good, but praise isn't easy. As we said, we have a tendency to be self-absorbed and to revert to habitual forms of praying and praising, where we use the same words again and again. This means that we need at least a few methods to meaningfully incorporate worship into our prayers.

First, we can make use of the Psalms when we pray. Our own words of praise quickly run dry, so we should use the inspired words of the Psalms for our doxologies to the Father, Son, and Holy Spirit. Have the Psalms open and pray them, echoing their words even as Jesus did in his perfect prayer.

Second, we should have open eyes for what the triune God has done and is doing, every day of our lives. Take note of his many good gifts—write them down if necessary—and then bring them before him in thanksgiving and praise. Recalling God's faithfulness strengthens our prayers, for we see that he has never let us down and never ignored our cries.

Third, combine prayer with any Scripture that you have recently read. Many believers read a portion of the Bible just before they pray, at mealtimes or at bedtime. This is a commendable practice, and we should let this Bible reading give shape to our praise. Reflect for a moment on what God has revealed about himself in his word, and then take time to glorify him for this perfection in your prayer. It is good to praise him, it is pleasant, and it is fitting!

Full Assurance

While we might sometimes neglect to praise God in our prayers, probably few of our prayers are ever lacking that final word: "Amen."

It's the first word many children learn when they start praying. Unless we nod off to sleep before we pray it, "Amen" is rarely missing. This would be wonderful if "Amen" was a magical word, a special word that suddenly gave our prayers their power—but it isn't, for "Amen" is just a word. As with any word, we can say it repeatedly and loudly, but if we don't mean it, it's not worth much at all—like the unrepentant "sorry" or the ungrateful "thank you."

When Jesus taught us to end our prayers with "Amen," he was teaching more than a way to announce that we're finished. "Amen" is related to the Hebrew word that describes something constant, dependable, and true. Similar to "Hallelujah," it is an Old Testament word that has now been absorbed into hundreds of languages. In prayer, it expresses our confidence in God. "Amen," we say—"it is true and certain." What Jesus teaches here is an attitude; he is encouraging a spirit in which we pray to the Father with full assurance of faith. This assurance means that whenever we offer up our prayers, we can do so in the confidence that God will hear and answer us.

Saying "Amen" has consequences for our prayers. It means we shouldn't pray just because it's expected, because it's what we've always done at meal times or bed times. And we shouldn't pray if we don't really believe these prayers are going to ascend to the heavenly throne-room of God. Rather, when we pray, we believe in the God who hears our voice. Sometimes we might be blasé about prayer, but God is not. Think of what James says of the righteous man's prayer: "Let him ask in faith, with no doubting, for the one who doubts is like a wave of the sea that is driven and tossed by the wind" (1:6). Not doubting God, not tuning God out, but firmly believing—*that's* how to pray. And when we do pray in faith, "Amen" is more than a word; in a beautiful way, "Amen" expresses our confidence in God our Father. We say it with force, with conviction, with meaning: "Amen."

"Amen and Amen!"

The closing of Psalm 41 resounds with the wonderful doxology—
"Blessed be the LORD, the God of Israel, from everlasting to everlasting!" (v. 13). This is followed with not just one "Amen," but a
double declaration of confidence: "Amen and Amen" (v. 13). This
verse is one of the "seams" or "joints" of the Psalter. It seems that,
at some point in Israel's past, an editor collected all the Psalms in
one place. The 150 Psalms were placed into five separate books,
probably meant to correspond to the five books of Moses (Genesis
through Deuteronomy). Psalms 1 to 41 is considered one book, 42
to 72 is another, 73 to 89 a third, 90 to 106 a fourth book, and 107
to 150 the last book within the Psalms.

The first four books end with God's people's emphatic statement of confidence in God: "Amen and Amen." Each book ends
with the worshiper wanting to underline everything that has been
said, all the praise and confession and petition and thanksgiving:
"It is true and certain." Those who know God's daily grace should
pray with many "Amens" in their hearts. Because God is God, our
prayers should not be feeble or uncaring or insincere, but filled
with confidence: "You have upheld me . . . and set me in your presence forever" (Ps 41:12).

A Resolute Confidence

Jesus and the Psalms teach us to pray with resolute confidence and
firm conviction. Yet even we who believe in the power of prayer
sometimes give up praying too quickly. For instance, if there is a
need in our church or distress about world events, we shouldn't
just mention the issue in prayer once, and then no more. Praying
with confidence means persistently laying our needs and burdens
before the Lord, believing that he hears us: "In the day of trouble
the LORD delivers" (Ps 41:1). Similarly, if we are troubled by a
situation of brokenness and hurt in our family or church, we might
pray but without a firm hope or expectation. "Too bad it won't make
a difference," we think, "It's essentially an impossible situation. I'll

pray, but I would be really surprised if anything changes." Here too, we must remember that our prayers are offered to the God who hears and who answers, the one who has all the power and glory and whose kingdom is over all.

When our eyes are open to God's true greatness, we will have a growing confidence in prayer. We say "Amen" because we're confident that the almighty God can heal the sick. We say "Amen" because we're confident that the Father will forgive our sins and is able to provide for all our physical needs. We're convinced that Christ can build the church, save the lost, and bring back those who stray. Perhaps God will make us wait, or perhaps his answer will look much different than we expect. Yet we are confident that our God will never ignore us. With our "Amen," we speak to God from the heart, certain that he will hear our prayer for the sake of Christ. This is the key to prayer, and the power of prayer: because of his Son, our Savior, God our Father is able and willing to hear and answer. In ourselves we are nothing, and we deserve nothing, but God hears us for the sake of Christ.

In this connection, it is right to recall again how God answered our prayers in the past. "Remember when I prayed for this blessing, and the way God heard me? Remember how we were so worried, and how the Lord took care of us? Remember asking for his grace in that trial, and how God provided?" In the moment of anxious pleading, we might have felt like the friend at midnight, desperate in the dark, nearly hopeless, banging on the door with a heavy heart (Luke 11:5–8). But God answered. We didn't necessarily receive a multitude of things, but the Lord came near in his grace, and he provided what was needed. And so he always will, just as he promised.

Amen in Christ

In 2 Corinthians 1:20, Paul calls Jesus the "Amen" to our prayers. He writes, "For all the promises of God find their Yes in him. That is why it is through him that we utter our Amen to God for his glory." This means that whatever God has promised, he will also grant because of Christ. Has the Father promised you a knowledge of his will? Yes. Has he promised the complete forgiveness of all your sins? Yes. Has God promised your daily bread? Yes. Has he promised a place in his eternal kingdom? Yes. Has the Father promised you sufficient grace for purity, for faith, for service? Yes, yes, and yes! He has promised, so freely ask for all these things, asking without doubting and without ceasing. If we petition our Father in Christ for anything he promised in his word, we can be certain that we will receive. This knowledge gives our prayers great strength of purpose, a confidence that turns our feeble words into holy messages that are delivered straight into the throne-room of God.

Because of Jesus, we have no reason to stop praying. We have no reason to neglect prayer, or to hurry through prayer, whether at the beginning or the middle or the end of a day. Rather, in Jesus's blood we have every reason to ask boldly for God's blessings. We have every reason to persistently and confidently pray to the Father—for God has promised us his precious gifts in Christ! As we close our prayers, let us speak with joyful praise and firm confidence. For it is true and certain: the God to whom we pray is our Father, and his love toward us will endure forever. For Jesus's sake, we may conclude our prayers with this fitting finale from Psalm 41: "Blessed be the LORD, the God of Israel, from everlasting to everlasting! Amen and Amen."

Reflection and Discussion Questions

1. How do you tend to conclude your prayers? In what ways could you improve?

2. A doxology-filled prayer not only glorifies God, it also encourages the one who is praying. Reflect on how this is true.

3. This chapter suggested a few ways for you to learn the language of praise. What else could you do to build more doxology into your prayers?

4. What can you learn about the word "Amen" from Deuteronomy 27:15-26?

5. Are you always able to end your prayers with an assured "Amen"? Why or why not?

6. Reflect on Hebrews 10:19-22. How does the finished work of Christ give you confidence in prayer?

Conclusion

Pray without Ceasing

LONG BEFORE YOU DECIDED to read this book, you had probably established some good habits of prayer. Many Christians pray at mealtimes, unless we're really in a hurry and need to get going. Likely we pray at our bedtimes too, unless we're really tired and we fall asleep before we do. Quite certainly we pray when worried about something or when facing a sudden crisis. Regular times for prayer are commendable, and it is entirely fitting that prayer is our response to life's anxieties and troubles. But then we should listen again to the injunction from 1 Thessalonians 5:17 which we heard near the beginning of this book, where the Holy Spirit includes a simple but complicating element with his instruction. He doesn't just say "Pray," but he says, "Pray *without ceasing*." Of all the words that he could've added, these are certainly the most challenging: pray—not regularly, or consistently, or at least five times per day—pray "without ceasing."

This is challenging and humbling, because far from praying continually, we often forget to pray. The excuses hardly need rehearsing: life is too busy, there are too many distractions, we were too tired, or we simply forgot. Other times we think there is no necessity for prayer because everything in our life seems to carry on well enough without asking for God's blessing. Yet the Lord, knowing our critical need and loving us deeply, commands us: "Pray without ceasing."

We should be clear about what this command means, because some readers are probably clearing their throats already, preparing to object that it is impossible to be praying all the time. How *could* we? We still have work to do, after all, and we need to sleep and eat. But God is saying that we ought to saturate our days with prayer. Praying continually means that while we go through our day, we are always just a moment away from prayer. While driving to work, while baking bread, while settling into the classroom, while fueling up the car, while washing the dishes, while walking down the corridor—we are ready to commune with our heavenly Father. Perhaps with a few words of quiet intercession for the people who come to our mind; with a brief thanksgiving for the Father's good gifts; with a whisper of wonder at the amazing work that Christ is doing in his church; with an urgent call for the Holy Spirit's guidance—we may and we should pray at any time.

Rather than having God distant from our thoughts other than briefly at mealtimes and bedtimes and calamities, praying continually is always being ready to enter the presence of the Father in order to speak with him. Prayer should be an essential building block for each day as we live every hour in dependence on God. We are poor and needy, but he is mighty and gracious. May our prayer-saturated life be the constant acknowledgement that God has everything to do with everything that we do! Let unceasing prayer be our humble confession that in God we live and move and have our being (Acts 17:28).

A sinner's prayer is incapable of anything in itself, for it is just a stringing together of weak words and not worthy of any attention. But these modest words have a legitimate message and a genuine power, because when we pray, we do so through Jesus Christ—and what a privilege that we may! We are sinners who once were alienated from the life of God, but through his Son we have been brought back into the joy of fellowship and friendship. Whenever we choose to pray, there is a beautiful display of the restored bond between God and us.

Think of two people who were no longer on speaking terms, perhaps a husband and wife on the brink of divorce. For whatever reason, even something as simple as communication between them has come to a grinding halt. Instead there is only a lot of mute resentment which periodically erupts into a shouting match, followed by more days of stony silence. But then there is reconciliation, forgiveness, and a newfound peace. And now the thing they delight to do is *talk*. After months—maybe years—of quiet animosity, they open up, they share, and slowly the relationship begins to thrive again. This is a faint picture of our relationship with God. Where there used to be animosity and a looming condemnation, by God's grace in Jesus there is now peace between us and him. Now we can ask, seek, and knock—and in response the Father opens himself to us (Luke 11:9–10)! The heart of prayer isn't about *what* we get, it's about *who* we get. We get God, the warmth of his love and fellowship and grace in Jesus Christ.

Even in the times when we must wait patiently for God's answer, or when we have not at all received what we've prayed for, God's will is that we pray "without ceasing." We keep praying, for the relationship between him and us has not changed: in Christ he is still our faithful Father in heaven, he still knows exactly what we need every day, and he is certainly going to keep his loving promise to provide (Matt 6:32–33). Such are the lessons of the Scripture-soaked petitions and praises of the Lord's Prayer. They encourage us to voice with renewed appreciation the perfect prayer that Jesus taught, to continually seek God with deep reverence, firm confidence, and loyal love. To God our Father, this is our unceasing prayer: "Hallowed be your name. Amen and Amen!"

Bibliography

Allen, Leslie C. *Psalms 101–150*. Revised Edition. Word Biblical Commentary 21. Grand Rapids, MI: Zondervan, 2015.

Chapell, Bryan. *Praying Backwards: Transform Your Prayer Life by Beginning in Jesus' Name*. Grand Rapids: Baker, 2005.

Craigie, Peter C., and Marvin E. Tate. *Psalms 1–50*. Rev. ed. Word Biblical Commentary 19. Grand Rapids: Zondervan, 2016.

Goldingay, John. *Psalms*. 3 vols. Baker Commentary on the Old Testament Wisdom and Psalms 4–6. Grand Rapids: Baker, 2006–08.

Keller, Timothy. *Prayer: Experiencing Awe and Intimacy with God*. London: Hodder & Stoughton, 2016.

Millar, J. Gary. *Calling on the Name of the Lord*. New Studies in Biblical Theology 38. Downers Grove: InterVarsity, 2016.

Miller, Paul E. *A Praying Life: Connecting with God in a Distracting World*. Colorado Springs: NavPress, 2009.

Packer, J. I. *Praying the Lord's Prayer*. Wheaton: Crossway, 2007.

Ryken, Philip. *When You Pray: Making the Lord's Prayer Your Own*. Philipsburg: Presbyterian & Reformed, 2006.

Sproul, R. C. *The Prayer of the Lord*. Lake Mary, FL: Reformation Trust, 2018.

Spurgeon, Charles. *The Power of Christ's Prayer Life*. Edited by Lance Wubbels. Lynnwood, WA: Emerald, 1995.

Tate, Marvin. *Psalms 51–100*. Word Biblical Commentary 20. Grand Rapids: Zondervan, 2015.

Underwood, Don. *Pray Like Jesus: Rediscovering the Lord's Prayer*. Nashville: Abingdon, 2017.

Whitney, Donald S. *Praying the Bible*. Wheaton: Crossway, 2015.

Yancey, Philip. *Prayer: Does it Make Any Difference?* Grand Rapids: Zondervan, 2006.

Scripture Index

Made in United States
North Haven, CT
12 January 2023

30922227R00075